Vol. numbers appear first (in bold) followed by page numbers, a change in volume is preceded by a semi-colon. You can also find this title list at the back of the book.

Vol. 177 Crime in the UK
Vol. 182 Teenage Conceptions
Vol. 183 Work and Employment
Vol. 185 Student Matters
Vol. 186 Cannabis Use
Vol. 188 Tobacco and Health
Vol. 189 The Homeless Population
Vol. 190 Coping with Depression
Vol. 191 The Changing Family
Vol. 192 Bereavement and Grief
Vol. 193 Endangered Species
Vol. 194 Responsible Drinking
Vol. 195 Alternative Medicine
Vol. 196 Censorship Issues
Vol. 197 Living with Disability
Vol. 198 Sport and Society
Vol. 199 Self-Harming and Suicide
Vol. 200 Sustainable Transport
Vol. 201 Mental Wellbeing
Vol. 202 Child Exploitation
Vol. 203 The Gambling Problem
Vol. 204 The Energy Crisis
Vol. 205 Nutrition and Diet
Vol. 206 Coping with Stress

Vol. 207 Consumerism and Ethics
Vol. 208 Genetic Modification
Vol. 209 Education and Society
Vol. 210 The Media
Vol. 211 Biotechnology and Cloning
Vol. 212 International Terrorism
Vol. 213 The Armed Forces
Vol. 214 Vegetarian Diets
Vol. 215 Religion in Society
Vol. 216 Tackling Climate Change
Vol. 217 Euthanasia and Assisted Suicide
Vol. 218 A Sustainable Future
Vol. 219 Class and Social Mobility
Vol. 220 Population Growth and Migration
Vol. 221 Equality and Gender Roles
Vol. 222 Tourism and Travel
Vol. 223 Crime. Punishment and Justice
Vol. 224 Domestic and Relationship Abuse
Vol. 225 LGBT Equality
Vol. 226 Globalisation and Trade
Vol. 227 Ethics in Business
Vol. 228 Illegal Drug Use
Vol. 229 Protecting Human Rights
Vol. 230 Evolution of the Internet

Vol. 231 The Abortion Debate
Vol. 232 Bullying in our Society
Vol. 233 Exploring Animal Rights
Vol. 234 Skin Deep - debating body image
Vol. 235 The Poverty Crisis
Vol. 236 Racial Discrimination
Vol. 237 Discussing Sexual Health
Vol. 238 Sexualising Society
Vol. 239 Ageing and the Elderly
Vol. 240 Citizenship in the UK
Vol. 241 Understanding Fitness
Vol. 242 Global Waste
Vol. 243 Understanding AIDS & HIV
Vol. 244 Marriage and Partnership
Vol. 245 Privacy in the UK
Vol. 246 The Sex Trade
Vol. 247 Fertility and Reproduction
Vol. 248 Discussing Child Abuse
Vol. 249 Eating Disorders
Vol. 250 Understanding Finance
Vol. 251 National Health Issues
Vol. 252 Adolescent Health
Vol. 253 The Housing Crisis

Titles of publications are in *italics*

10:23 campaign against homeopathy **195**.31, 32
12 Step programmes **203**.25
4G mobile spectrum **230**.1
40 Days for Life campaign **231**.34, 35

A&E departments
    and self-harm **199**.13-14
    waiting times **251**.17
A-levels (Advanced Level)
    as predictor of degree performance **209**.12;
    219.32
abortion **231**.1-39
    aborted fetuses in stem cell trials **211**.33
    alternatives to **231**.8, 17-18
    anti-abortion campaigns **231**.34-5
    arguments against (pro-life) **231**.1, 16
    arguments for (pro-choice) **231**.1, 16
    counselling **231**.24-5, 26-9, 31, 36-7
    and disability **231**.20
    effects **231**.5, 6-7
        on men **231**.9
        on mental health **231**.14-15
    ethical issues **231**.16-29
    and the law **231**.1-2, 3, 32
    private clinics
        and advertising **231**.38
        and counseling **231**.24-5
        gender abortion **231**.30-31
        NHS funding **231**.24
    procedure **231**.6-7
    reasons for abortions **231**.13, 32
    religious positions on **231**.19
    risks **231**.6-7
    sex-selection abortion **231**.18, 30-31
    statistics **182**.2, 29; **231**.10-12

and teenage pregnancies **182**.2, 12-13, 29
    making the decision **182**.6, 9
    time limit **231**.21-3
Abortion Act 1967 **231**.1
absenteeism
    sickness absence **183**.8, 9
    and work-life balance **183**.17
absolute poverty **235**.1, 2-3
abuse
    and children's mental health **201**.3
    class-based **219**.5-6
    elder abuse **239**.34
    racist abuse
        in football **236**.9, 12, 13, 15, 38, 39
        on Twitter **236**.31
    trafficked children **202**.29
    see also domestic abuse; emotional abuse;
neglect; physical abuse; sexual abuse
abusers
    child abusers **248**.6, 26
    domestic, help for **224**.39
academic achievement *see* educational
achievement
academic learning style in schools **209**.2
academic qualifications
    versus vocational qualifications
        see also exams
Academies Programme **209**.25, 26
    and social mobility **219**.28
access rights, disabled people
    to goods and services **197**.21, 25
    public transport **197**.23
    to work **197**.21, 24
access to children *see* contact
Access to Work **197**.21
accidents
    road accidents **200**.12
achievement *see* educational achievement
acidification of oceans **193**.30
ACPO Child Protection Delivery Plan **248**.36
acquired immunodeficiency syndrome *see* AIDS
active euthanasia **217**.5

Acts of Union **240**.32
adaptive dysfunction **197**.6
Adele, on cover of *Vogue* **234**.6
addictions
    cannabis **186**.1, 10-11, 29
    Facebook **230**.15
    gambling **203**.6, 20
      see also problem gambling
    Internet **230**.14, 16-18
    nicotine **188**.10, 16
    pornography **246**.1-2
    shopping **207**.6
    smoking **252**.38
Additional Member System **240**.29
additives see food additives
ADD see attention deficit disorder
additional paternity leave **221**.4-5
adoption **182**.6, 8-9; **191**.18-25; **247**.14-17
    adopted children and education **247**.17
    adoption leave and pay **183**.18; **247**.16
    adoption process **191**.18-19; **247**.15
    as alternative to abortion **231**.8, 17-18
    contact with birth family **247**.16
    of obese children **241**.23
    same-sex couples **191**.22-5; **225**.34
Adoption of Children Act 1926 **248**.35
adult children
    living with parents **191**.26
    supported by parents **191**.27-8
adult learners **209**.39
adult stem cells **211**.28, 29
adultery as grounds for divorce **244**.30
advance decisions (medical treatment) **217**.13, 35-6
advance statements **217**.35
Adventist Health Study 2 **214**.31-2
advertising
    abortion clinics **231**.38
    and age **196**.20
    airbrushing and unrealistic body images **234**.24-6, 27-8
    alcohol **194**.39
    and children **207**.35-6, 37, 39; **234**.23
    junk food **205**.38
    media advertising spending **210**.15
    online **230**.5
    and pressure to spend **250**.32
    regulation and body confidence issues **234**.21
    sexual services **246**.23
    and sexualized imagery **238**.5, 6-7
    tobacco **188**.23
    using disabled model **197**.10
aerobic activity **241**.25
aesthetic surgery see cosmetic surgery
affluence see wealth
affordable home ownership schemes **253**.6, 7-8, 9
affordable housing construction **253**.28
Afghanistan conflict after death of Osama bin Laden **212**.24-5
Africa
    AIDS strategy support **243**.29
    child soldiers **202**.33, 37-9
    criminalization of homosexuality **225**.39
    gender inequality **221**.1

HIV/AIDS infection rates **243**.26, 27
    older people with HIV **243**.20
    poverty rates **235**.23, 24
    press freedom **196**.2
African communities, attitudes to HIV/AIDS **243**.16-17
African people and HIV risk **243**.8
age
    and advertising **196**.20
    and alcohol consumption **194**.1-2, 30
    and alcohol-related deaths **194**.13
    and career fulfillment **183**.6
    and child labour **202**.3, 16
    and child soldiers **202**.33-4
    and childhood aggression **224**.23
    of criminal responsibility **223**.30, 31-2
    and depression **190**.5, 22-3
    at divorce **191**.8
    in domestic violence definition **224**.35-6
    and drinking behaviour, young people **194**.2
    and eating disorders
    and eating disorders **249**.4
    and fertility **247**.2, 4, 5, 6
    of first drink **194**.3
    of first sexual intercourse **182**.1
    of foetal viability **231**.21, 22
    IVF and older women **247**.10, 22-5
    at marriage **191**.1
    retirement age **183**.14-15
    of smokers **188**.1
    voting age lowering **240**.30-31
age of consent **202**.16
age discrimination **239**.4, 8, 12-13
    in home care **229**.33
    NHS ban **239**.11
    against young people **239**.6-7
age limits for gambling, children's knowledge of **203**.13
age ratings
    music videos **238**.5
    video games **196**.17
age structure of population, global **220**.8
ageing **239**.1-39
    ageing experience, international comparisons **239**.8-9
    ageing process **239**.1-2
    costs of ageing population **239**.15
    and health **239**.3-4, 24-39
    lesbian, gay and bisexual people **239**.10-11
    people with HIV **243**.19-20, 30-31
    stereotypes **239**.4-5
    young peoples' attitudes to **239**.6-7
    see also older people
ageing population
    global **220**.8; **239**.3, 4, 13
    UK **239**.15, 16
ageism see age discrimination
Agenda 21 and waste management **242**.4
agentist capitalism **226**.22, 23
aggressive behaviour in children **224**.22-3
agoraphobia **252**.14
agriculture
    and animal welfare **233**.2, 3

Annual Index 2013

Series Editor: Cara Acred

Complete A-Z index listings for all
70 *ISSUES* titles currently in print

30130504320763

Independence Educational Publishers

First published by Independence Educational Publishers

The Studio, High Green

Great Shelford

Cambridge CB22 5EG

England

© Independence 2013

British Library Cataloguing in Publication Data

Annual index 2013. -- (Issues)

1. Issues--Indexes. 2. Social problems--Indexes.

I. Series II. Acred, Cara editor of compilation.

016.3'61-dc23

ISBN-13: 9781861686640

Printed in Great Britain

MWL Print Group Ltd

and climate change **216**.11
cotton farming **202**.13-14
environmental impact **214**.16, 17, 22-3
factory farming **233**.3, 7-8
fairtrade *see* fair trade
fur farming **233**.18, 19
mega-farms **233**.3, 9-11
subsidies, impact on developing countries **226**.33
sustainable meat production **214**.14, 20-21, 23
waste produce harvested for charities **242**.39
see also animal welfare; food production;
genetically modified (GM) crops; organic farming
aid
aid for trade **226**.34
definitions **235**.32
effectiveness **235**.31-2
and gay rights **225**.14
and slums **235**.38
AIDS (Acquired Immune Deficiency Syndrome)
AIDS-related deaths **243**.6, 26, 27
definition **243**.1
global targets **243**.26-7
government health campaign (1986) **251**.2
symptoms **243**.2-3
timeline **243**.7
treatments *see* antiretroviral therapy (ART)
see also HIV (Human Immunodeficiency Virus)
air pollution *see* emissions
air travel
air passenger duty tax **222**.14-15
disabled people **197**.12
emissions from **200**.14, 24
environmental impact **200**.24-5
airbrushing and body image **234**.5, 18, 24-6, 27-8
aircraft carriers and defence budget cuts **213**.21
al-Qaida
and Afghanistan conflict **212**.24-5
after death of Osama bin Laden **212**.23
terrorist attacks in Great Britain **212**.6
alcohol
advertising **194**.39
binge drinking *see* binge drinking
calorie content **205**.5
consumption
after divorce **244**.32
children **194**.25-6
elderly people **239**.33
myths **194**.16
reducing **194**.5, 16, 23
social drinkers **194**.17
women **194**.7
young people **194**.1-2; **252**.2, 31, 35
and crime **194**.19-20, 21, 29
deaths related to **194**.13
and domestic violence **224**.6
drink spiking **194**.8-10
drinking behaviour
binge drinking **194**.22-3
children **194**.25-6
and knowledge of safe drinking guidelines
194.34
social drinking **194**.17
young people **194**.2-3, 24

effects of **194**.6-7, 9, 22-3
on appearance **194**.6
on behaviour **194**.19-20
effects on others **194**.15, 27-8
and elderly people **239**.33
health benefits of **194**.18
health risks of **194**.6, 7, 15, 17, 18
binge drinking **194**.22-3
mental health effects **194**.6
social drinking **194**.17
young people **194**.19
and hydration **205**.28
and the law
24-hour drinking **194**.20
see also drink-driving
and pregnancy **194**.14
and sex **237**.3
and smoking **188**.10
and stress **206**.33
and students **185**.9, 10
underage drinking **194**.1-3, 25
see also young people and alcohol
units of **194**.4-5, 14
recommended limits **194**.8, 14, 18
see also binge drinking; young people and
alcohol
alcohol abuse **194**.22-39
and crime **194**.21, 29
effects on family **194**.27-8
help **194**.23
and homeless people **189**.10-11, 13
and mental illness **201**.17
risks **194**.22-3, 27-8
signs of **194**.30
statistics **194**.30
alcohol-related brain impairment **201**.10
alien invasive species **193**.12
UK **193**.38-9
allergies and food additives **205**.15
alternative medicine **195**.1-39
buying habits **195**.8
definition **195**.1
herbal medicines **195**.9-13
reasons for using **195**.5, 6-7
safety **195**.2
types **195**.3-5
see also homeopathy
alternative tourism **222**.16
definition **222**.24
see also ecotourism; voluntourism
Alternative Vote (AV) **240**.29
Alzheimer's disease **239**.24, 28
and animal research **233**.36
Alzheimer's Society **201**.11
Amazon forest destruction and cattle ranching
193.14
Amazon town banning tourists **222**.32
Americas, press freedom **196**.2
amino acids and GM food **208**.20
Amnesty International, response to UK counter-
terrorism review **212**.38-9
Amy Winehouse Foundation **228**.10-11
anabolic steroids **198**.29-30; **228**.26

anaerobic digestion plant for food waste **242**.38
anal sex **237**.4
    and conception **182**.4
analgesics **198**.28-9
anger management **199**.6; **206**.3
Anglican Church and abortion **231**.19
animal cloning **211**.7-21
    Dolly the sheep **211**.7, 8
    ethical concerns **211**.10-11
    for food production **211**.6, 10-19
Animal Defenders International **233**.4
animal experimentation **233**.3, 28-39
    alternatives to **233**.28, 32
    and animal welfare societies **233**.1
    arguments against **233**.35-6
    arguments for **233**.37-8
    and genetically modified animals **211**.37-8
    myths and facts **233**.30-33
    reasons for **233**.28
    regulation of **233**.28, 33
    types of animals used **233**.29, 33
animal fights **233**.6, 17, 27
animal rights
    whales and dolphins **233**.20-21
    see also animal welfare
animal welfare **233**.1-6
    circuses **233**.14-15
    and cloning **211**.10, 19
    and farming **233**.7-11
    and fur trade **233**.3-4, 18-19
    UK legislation on **233**.1-2, 5-6
    and vegetarianism **214**.5
Animal Welfare Act **233**.2, 5-6
    and film classification **196**.14
animals
    genetic modification *see* genetically modified
animals
    homosexual behaviour **225**.15
anniversaries and grief **192**.5, 10, 20
anorexia athletica **249**.7
anorexia nervosa **249**.1, 6
    causes **249**.32
    causing death of model **234**.36
    effects **249**.32, 35
    force feeding of patient **249**.38-9
    mealtime support **249**.37
    treatment **249**.33
Antabuse **203**.27
Antarctic ice sheet and climate change **216**.12
anti-abortion campaigns **231**.34-5
anti-bullying policies
    schools **232**.18
    and sexuality **232**.15
anti-bullying strategies **232**.3-4, 16, 19-21
    cyberbullying **232**.26-7, 28, 29, 39
    schools **232**.3, 10, 18
anti-depressant drugs **190**.10-11, 32-3; **206**.3
    and anxiety **206**.13
    for children and young people **252**.19
    and bipolar disorder **190**.10-11
    having little effect on mild depression **190**.36
    and seasonal affective disorder **190**.7
    and suicide **190**.24

    see also drug treatments for depression
anti-discrimination legislation **183**.13
anti-gay abuse, football **198**.26
anti-Muslim   hate crime **215**.28-30; **236**.14, 24
    see also Islamophobia
anti-pornography campaign **246**.6
anti-psychotic drugs **190**.10
anti-racism laws *see* legislation and racism
anti-Semitism **215**.36
    football chants **236**.39
anti-social behaviour and alcohol **194**.19-20
Anti-Social Behaviour Orders and prostitution
    246.21, 25
anti-terrorism *see* counter-terrorism
Anti-terrorism Crime and Security Act 2001 **212**.19
anti-vivisection societies **233**.1
antibiotic use in farming **233**.7
anticipated stigma about HIV **243**.16-17
antiretroviral therapy (ART) **243**.3-4
    curing baby born with HIV **243**.37-9
    worldwide access to **243**.6
anxiety **206**.10-15; **252**.13-15
    causes **206**.11-12
    definition **206**.10, 14
    medication **206**.13
    and mortality **190**.20
    symptoms of **206**.10-11
appearance
    effects of alcohol **194**.6
    young smokers' concerns **188**.14
apprenticeships **183**.29, 38; **209**.38
    gender segregation **221**.28
approved mental health professionals **201**.38
aptitude tests for university admission **219**.32
Arab Spring and human rights violations **229**.9
architecture of the home and privacy **245**.2
Armed Forces **213**.1-39
    Armed Forces Covenant **213**.25-7, 28
    Army life **213**.1-2
    deaths **213**.9
    ex-service personnel *see* ex-service personnel
    injured personnel **213**.7, 8-9, 10-11
    and mental health **213**.3-6
    post traumatic stress disorder **213**.3-4, 5, 34
    restructuring **213**.17-19, 22-3
    and sexual orientation, USA **225**.38-9
    Strategic Defence and Security Review **213**.17-21
    Territorial Army **213**.30
    and women **213**.12-14
    and young people **213**.15-16
arranged marriages **244**.12
arrests
    British nationals overseas **222**.15
    at football matches **198**.13
Article 8, Human Rights Act **245**.1
ASBOs (Anti-Social Behaviour Orders) and
    prostitution **246**.21, 25
ash from waste incinerators **242**.36
Asia
    child soldiers **202**.33
    criminalization of homosexuality **225**.39
    poverty rates **235**.23, 24, 25
Asia-Pacific region, press freedom **196**.2

Asian people
    British identity **240**.6
    in football **198**.24
Assange, Julian (WikiLeaks) **210**.20-21
assaults on school staff **209**.16
assisted dying
    arguments for **217**.38-9
    legislation **217**.2
    see also assisted suicide; euthanasia
Assisted Dying for the Terminally Ill bill **217**.2
assisted reproductive technologies (ART) *see* fertility treatments
assisted suicide **217**.5
    arguments against **217**.3-4
    arguments for **217**.3
    cases **217**.20, 21
    and disabled people **199**.39
    doctors' opposition to **217**.22
    legal guidelines **199**.37-8
    physician-assisted suicide **217**.22, 24-5
    prevalence in UK **217**.24-5
    public attitudes to **217**.23, 34
    see also assisted dying; euthanasia
asthma **252**.7
    and exercise **198**.23
astro-tourism **222**.17-18
asylum seekers
    destitution **189**.14-15
    young,and mental health problems **201**.2
asymmetric federalism **240**.28
atheists, protesting against religious faith **196**.11-12
athletes
    drinking behaviour of stars, effect on young people **198**.14
    and drugs *see* drugs in sport
    and eating disorders **249**.16
    foreign born athletes in British Olympic team **240**.10-11
    punishment for missing drugs tests **198**.39
    talent identification **198**.8-10, 22
Attendance Allowance **197**.32-4
audio media trends, international **210**.15
Australia
    health care **251**.9
    Internet censorship **196**.30
    transgender rights **225**.24
aversion therapy for homosexual behaviour **225**.16
aviation *see* air travel
Avon Foundation **227**.21

babies
    born with HIV **243**.1-2, 26-7
        cured of HIV **243**.37-9
        life as teenagers **243**.23-5
    physical activity guidelines **241**.6
    premature, viability **231**.21, 22
Baby P **248**.1
bail, in Legal Aid, Sentencing and Punishment of Offenders Bill **223**.25

Bailey Review on Sexualisation of childhood **238**.2, 5-7, 8, 33, 34
balance of excellence, sport **198**.37
balanced diet *see* healthy eating
banana trade **226**.35
Bangkok climate change negotiations **216**.37
Bangladesh, girls' education **244**.15
banks
    bail-outs **227**.16
    customer attitudes **250**.7, 8
    informing of a death **192**.32
    student accounts **185**.2-3
    taxation **235**.13-15
    use of tax havens **227**.36
Barbie body image **234**.31
bariatric (weight loss) surgery
    cost effectiveness **241**.18
    for teenagers **241**.22
barristers, ethnic minorities **236**.12
batteries, potato-powered **204**.39
battery farmed chickens **233**.3, 7
BBC
    Choosing to Die documentary **217**.20
    Editorial Guidelines **210**.27
    Ofcom regulation **196**.20
    radio and TV services **210**.3
BDD *see* body dysmorphic disorder
bears, reintroduction into Britain **193**.33-4
beauty pageants for children **238**.28-30
beavers, reintroduction into Britain **193**.34
bed and breakfast hotels, homeless families **189**.8
bees, declining numbers **193**.27-8
begging **189**.18-20
    giving to beggars **189**.35-6
behaviour
    effects of alcohol **194**.19-20, 23
    effects of sexual abuse **248**.4, 26
    pupils, and teacher stress **209**.15
    signs of drug use **228**.15
    stress and behavioural changes **206**.19
Belgium, euthanasia **217**.2, 32
benefits *see* state benefits
benign ignorance (indirect racism) **236**.28
benzoic acid **205**.14
bereavement **192**.1-39
    children **192**.4, 5-6,9-19, 21; **201**.2
    complicated **192**.16-17
    feelings **192**.1-2, 3, 9-10, 11
    funerals **192**.30-31, 34-7
    memorial websites **192**.38-9
    parents **192**.20-23
    practical matters **192**.24-39
    support **192**.2, 4, 5-6
        children **192**.4, 5, 10, 17
        young people **192**.10, 12, 17
    young people **192**.9-19
Bergen Facebook Addiction Scale **230**.15
Berlin Patient **243**.32, 33
betting **203**.4
    see also gambling
Bevan, Aneurin **219**.12
Big Issue **189**.37-9
Big Society **240**.33-4

bigamy **244**.3
binge drinking **194**.22-3
    effects **194**.22-3
    young people **252**.36
binge eating disorder **249**.2, 6-7
bingo **203**.4
bioaccumulative chemicals **193**.16
Bio-Bug (methane-powered car) **204**.39
biochemical causes of depression **190**.2
biodegradable products, environmental impact **218**.37
biodiesel, from algae **204**.34
biodiversity
    conservation, marine environments **218**.22-3
    and ecotourism **222**.28
    and global economy **193**.10-12
    key scientific questions **193**.7
    loss **193**.13; **218**.14, 18
        England **193**.31-2
    and oil palm industry **193**.8-9
    public attitudes to **216**.11; **218**.17
    and tourism **222**.22-3, 28
    value of **193**.6
bioenergy *see* biomass energy
bio-fortification **208**.19
biofuels **204**.3, 26, 32, 39; **208**.22
    from algae **204**.34
biological causes of criminal behaviour **223**.11
biomass heating **204**.3, 36
biomaterials **208**.21
biometrics **245**.33
biotech companies **208**.3-4, 24
biotechnology
    applications **211**.4
    definition **211**.1, 4
    history **211**.2-3
    see also cloning; genetic modification
bipolar affective disorder (manic depression) **185**.8; **190**.2, 8-11, 22; **201**.14-15, 24-5
    causes **190**.9
    diagnosis **190**.8
    experiences of sufferers **201**.14-15
    genetic factors **190**.11, 12-13
    prevalence **190**.23
    symptoms **190**.8-9
    treatments **190**.10-11
    types **190**.9-10
bird flu resistance, GM chickens **208**.14
birth control *see* contraception
birth rates
    and abortion rate, UK **231**.11
    global **220**.2, 4, 9, 13, 15
    and marital status **191**.1
    see also teenage pregnancies
bisexuality *see* LGBT people
Bishops in the House of Lords **215**.6
black people
    students, employment prospects **236**.19-20
    women and poverty **221**.34
    young people and mental health problems **201**.2
    see also employment and racism; ethnic
minorities; racism
Black Report on health care **251**.2

blessing ceremonies
    civil partnerships **244**.17
    marriages **244**.3
blindness, disability classification **197**.1
blogging **210**.16
blood, effects of smoking **188**.7
blood donation, from gay and bisexual men **225**.36-7
blood doping **198**.29
blood pressure
    effect of salt intake **205**.25
    high blood pressure **241**.4
blood products and HIV **243**.1
blood sugar and mental health **252**.25
blood tests
    drug testing in sport **198**.27
    for HIV diagnosis **243**.3
BMA
    and abortion counselling **231**.28, 29
    vote against homeopathy funding **195**.16
BMI *see* body mass index
BNP *see* British National Party
boardroom positions
    gender quotas **221**.16, 21
    women **221**.14, 15, 16, 17-18, 20, 21-2, 37
body confidence promotion
    Girlguiding UK **234**.34
    government campaign **234**.20-21, 37, 39
    parent pack **234**.39
    in schools **234**.11, 21, 29-30
body dysmorphic disorder/dysmorphophobia **249**.7
body image **234**.1-39
    Barbie ideal **234**.31
    and fashion industry **234**.5-6, 11
    improving **234**.1-3
    and the media **234**.5, 7, 8, 10, 11, 18
    men **234**.13, 16-17
    negative **234**.1
    and pornography **246**.1
    positive *see* body confidence promotion
    and young people **234**.7, 26
body mass index (BMI) **241**.14, 17; **249**.5
    and meat-eating **214**.35
body talk
    men **234**.16-17
    women **234**.8
body weight
    effects of eating breakfast **205**.9
    and fertility **247**.3, 5
    see also obesity; weight management
Bolivia
    child labour **202**.9-10
    education programme **229**.28
bones, effect of cannabis use **186**.6, 29
bonuses
    and inequality **227**.15
    justification of **227**.19
books, self-help, mental health **190**.38
borrowing *see* debt
botnets **196**.34
bottled waters, labelling rules **205**.11
bottom billion **235**.28-9
boxing, women **198**.19

boycotts, effect on child labour **202**.13
boys and young men
    and eating disorders **249**.17-19
    and education
        attitude to school **209**.11
        single-sex schools **221**.30
    gender stereotyping in boys' clothing **238**.1
    and parental separation **244**.36
    and parenthood **182**.17
    and sexual violence **238**.17
    stereotype pressures **238**.3
    toy preferences **221**.7-8
brain
    effects of ageing **239**.2
    effects of cannabis on **186**.28-9
    and placebo effect **195**.28-9
    and sexual orientation **225**.15-16
brain damage and gambling **203**.7
brain drain **220**.32-3
brands
    national versus store brands **207**.11
    ownership of ethical brands **207**.31
Brazil
    cattle ranching and deforestation **193**.14
    censorship of sexual content on the Internet
      196.37
    economic development **226**.20-21
    privacy rights **245**.4
    wellbeing of older people **239**.9
bread, labelling rules **205**.11-12
Break the Bag Habit campaign **242**.25
breakfast
    children going without **205**.8
    consumer habits **205**.17
    importance of **205**.9
breakfast clubs **205**.9
Breaking the Cycle Green Paper **223**.23
breast screening programme **251**.2
bribery and corruption in business **227**.31
bricks and walls layer of privacy **245**.2
Britain *see* UK
British Board of Film Classification (BBFC) **196**.13-
    16
    and legislation **196**.14
British Crime Survey **223**.3-5
British Heart Foundation and animal research
233.36
British Homeopathic Association **195**.22
British identity **240**.6, 8, 12-14
    ethnic minorities **240**.18-20
    Muslims **240**.17-18
    and national origins **240**.15-16
    and social group **240**.20
    and the Union Jack **240**.4-5
    Youth Parliament manifesto **240**.39
British Medical Association, vote against
homeopathy funding **195**.16
British National Party **236**.37
    inclusion in political debates **196**.7, 8
British tourists
    arrested or hospitalised overseas **222**.15
    holidaying at home **222**.5
Britishness *see* British identity

broadband services **230**.6-8
    super-fast broadband **210**.15
broadcasters
    freedom of expression **196**.24
    regulation **196**.18-20; **210**.27
    see also radio; television
Brook **237**.36
brothels
    and the law **246**.21-2
    legalisation **246**.26
Brown, Louise **247**.13
Brown, Timothy Ray (Berlin Patient) **243**.32, 33
Bt plants **208**.3, 21
Buddhism **215**.1
    and abortion **231**.19
    funerals **192**.36
    meditation as treatment for depression **190**.35-6
    and vegetarianism **214**.6
budgeting
    and debt repayment **250**.37-8
    students **185**.3, 11
Bulger, James **248**.35
bulimia nervosa **249**.1-2, 6, 18-19
    Amy Winehouse **249**.24
    diabetes sufferers **249**.11
    treatment **249**.33
bullfighting **233**.17
bullies
    characteristics of **232**.2
    consequences for **232**.22
bullying **232**.1-39
    children with gender-variant behaviour **225**.24
    cyber-bullying *see* cyberbullying
    dealing with bullying **232**.3, 17, 18, 19-21
      cyberbullying **232**.3, 26, 29, 39
      in the workplace **232**.23, 24
    and eating disorders **249**.21
    effects **232**.3, 8, 21, 22
      of cyberbullying **232**.25, 26
      on mental health **201**.2
    forms of bullying behaviour **232**.1, 21-2
    homophobic **225**.8, 9, 29; **232**.12-13, 15
    laws concerning **225**.7
      cyberbullying **232**.34-5, 37
    LGBT pupils **225**.8
    by mobile phone **232**.17, 25, 27, 29
    prevalence of **232**.30, 31
    punishment for **232**.22
    racist **232**.10, 11, 17; **236**.16
    reasons for **232**.2, 14, 25-6
    reporting **232**.20
      cyberbullying **232**.29, 36, 39
      workplace **232**.24
    sexual **221**.11
    signs of **232**.2-3
    and social media **227**.38; **232**.25, 26-7, 28
    statistics **232**.4
    and suicide **232**.9
    victims **232**.2, 8
    at work *see* workplace bullying
    see also bullies; school bullying; workplace
      bullying
burial abroad **192**.31

Burma, forced labour **229**.15
burqa wearing
 arguments for and against **215**.37-8
 prohibition in European countries **215**.34-6
 public opinions **215**.39
bursaries, students **185**.2; **250**.24
buses
 bus lane on M4 **200**.36
 and disabled people **197**.11-12
 electric **200**.28-9
 guided busways **200**.30, 32
 straddling bus **200**.29
 usage **200**.3
bushmeat trade **193**.23
business ownership aspirations **183**.7; **227**.6
businesses **227**.1-39
 corporate responsibility **227**.9-30
 and economic growth **227**.14
 and higher education **185**.34-6
 new working practices **227**.1-3
 public attitudes to **227**.13-14
 start-ups **227**.5
 statistics **227**.4-5, 6
 and tax **227**.32-6
butterflies, declining numbers, Britain **193**.36
buying a home
 disability rights **197**.21-2
 young people's difficulties **253**.203, 5
 see also home ownership

C4 rice **208**.20, 36
Cabinet, The **240**.26
Cadbury, accused of racist advertising **236**.29
CAES (Compressed Air Energy Storage) **204**.37-8
Cafcass (Children and Family Court Advisory and
Support Service) **248**.2, 35
calcium and vegetarian diets **214**.29, 30, 33
CALM (Campaign Against Living Miserably) **199**.28;
 252.15
Calthorpe Clinic, abortions **231**.30-31
Cambodia, child labour **202**.9
CAMbrella, research into complementary medicine
 195.16
camera development and privacy law **245**.2-3
Cameron, David
 entrepreneurship campaign **227**.7
 on immigration policy **220**.30-31
camping holidays, luxury **222**.20
Canada
 AIDS strategy support **243**.28
 as gap year destination **222**.19
 health care **251**.9
 seal hunting **233**.22, 23
cancer **239**.24
 and alcohol consumption **194**.6
 and cannabis use **186**.16, 15; **228**.9
 children and young people **252**.7-8
 and complementary therapies **195**.6-7
 as disability **197**.1

and passive smoking **188**.10-11
 and physical activity **241**.2
 and red meat consumption **214**.35
 and salt intake **205**.26
 and smoking **188**.8-11
 and vegetarian diets **214**.38-9
 see also cervical cancer; lung cancer
Cancer Research UK, funding animal research
 233.35, 38
Cancun Agreement **226**.4
Cancun climate change conference **216**.37, 39
cannabinoids
 THC **186**.7, 9, 13, 22
cannabis **186**.1-39
 appearance **186**.2
 cannabis oil **186**.2, 7, 22
 cannabis resin (hashish) **186**.2, 7, 9
 chemical content **186**.7, 9
 classification **186**.4-5, 32
  see also reclassification
 compulsive use **186**.11
 cost **186**.2
 cultivation
  method, effect on potency **186**.22
  sentencing guidelines **228**.30-31
 effects of **186**.1, 3,37-8, 9-10, 28-9; **228**.14
  on bones **186**.6, 29
  on the brain **186**.28-9
  cancer healing claims **186**.16; **228**.9
  on education and learning **186**.9-10
  on family life **186**.23-5
  on lungs **186**.15, 28
  medicinal **186**.16-17
  skunk **186**.13
 forms of **186**.2, 7, 9
 giving up **186**.11
 and hard drug use **186**.29
 herbal cannabis (marijuana/grass) **186**.2, 9
 history **186**.3-4, 7, 16-17, 25
 and the law **186**.1-2, 5, 8, 9, 30-39
 legalisation debate **186**.4, 38-9
 medicinal use of **186**.16-17
 and mental health **186**.10-13, 16, 28-9, 30, 31,
  32; **228**.8
 names for **186**.1
 penalties
  for possession **186**.1-2, 5, 9, 30
  sentencing guidelines **228**.28-9, 30-31
  for supply **186**.2, 30
 potency of **186**.2, 6, 21, 22
  skunk **186**.13
 psychosis **186**.10, 12, 31, 32
 purity **186**.2-3
 reclassification **186**.4-5, 32-3; 23
  public opinion **186**.31
 and schizophrenia **228**.8
 signs of use **228**.14
 THC (delta-9 tetrahydrocannabinol) **186**.7, 9, 13,
  22
 use
  giving up **186**.11
  worldwide **186**.18-19
canned hunting **193**.17

capitalism, defence of **227**.17, 18-19
car clubs **200**.11
car-free days **200**.19-20
carbon capture and storage **204**.27
carbon dioxide
    and GM crops **208**.20, 22
    rising levels, effects on oceans **193**.30
carbon dioxide emissions
    EU targets **204**.30
    and population growth **220**.14
    UK targets **204**.28-9
    see also greenhouse gas
carbon footprint, GM food **208**.29
carbon monoxide in tobacco smoke **188**.4, 7
carbon offsetting **216**.35-6
    and inequality **218**.3-4
    and rainforest protection **218**.20-21
cardiopulmonary resuscitation (CPR) **217**.13-14
cardiovascular disease (CVD)
    caused by stress **206**.4
    and eating red meat **214**.35
    incidence in UK **241**.2
    see also heart disease
care funding, personalization **197**.13
care leavers
    and homelessness **189**.6
    housing rights **189**.25
Care Quality Commission (CQC) **251**.26, 31
care services for older people
    concerns of lesbian, gay and bisexual people **239**.10-11
    funding **239**.20-23
    and human rights **229**.33-4
    need for **239**.4
cared-for children
    going missing **248**.28
and mental health problems **201**.3-4
career advice
    failing young people **183**.39
career aspirations, and gender **221**.21, 28-9
career breaks **183**.18, 20
career fulfillment age **183**.6
carers
    experiencing grief **192**.6
    young carers and neglect **248**.15
carrier bags *see* plastic bags
cars
    car clubs **200**.11
    congestion *see* congestion, traffic
    drink-driving *see* drink-driving
    electric **200**.26, 27; **204**.7
    emissions reduction **200**.15
    impact on health **200**.1, 23
    methane-powered **204**.39
    reducing use of **200**.7-8, 19-20, 25, 26
    sharing **200**.25
    see also driving; road accidents
cash payments **250**.3
casinos
    being sued for gambler's losses **203**.38
    casino games **203**.4
cassava, genetically modified **208**.36
cassiterite **226**.3

casual racism **236**.29-30
Catholic Church
    and abortion **231**.19, 39
    see also Christianity
cattle
    cloning **211**.12, 13-17
    ranching and deforestation **193**.14
    see also livestock farming
CBT *see* Cognitive Behavioural Therapy
CCTV (Closed Circuit Television) **245**.28-9
    and analysis of shopper behaviour **245**.35
    code of practice consultation **245**.32
    concerns about **245**.31
    public involvement in monitoring **245**.30
    rights to see footage **245**.29
    in schools **245**.36-7
celebrities
    and body image **234**.6-7
    and cyberbullying **232**.38
    in girls' magazines **238**.13
    and health advice **252**.5
    libel actions **210**.38
cell ageing **239**.1
censorship
    films **196**.13, 14
    and the Internet **196**.27-39
    sexual content on the Internet **196**.36-8
census, religious belief data **215**.5
centenarians **239**.1
Central African Republic **235**.39
Central and Eastern Europe, press freedom **196**.2
Centre for Appearance Research (CAR) **234**.4, 15
CEOP (Child Exploitation and Online Protection Centre) **248**.35
cerebral palsy **197**.3-4
cervical cancer **237**.28-9
    and HPV **237**.26
    screening **237**.27, 28, 32
    vaccination **237**.26-7, 28, 29-31
cetaceans' rights **233**.20-21
Chance to Shine cricket scheme **198**.3-4; **232**.7
charities
    animal welfare **233**.1
    and the Big Society **240**.34
    business support for **227**.20-21
    caring for wounded troops **213**.7
    fraud **207**.21, 22
    medical, funding animal research **233**.35-8
    poverty aid **235**.32
chatrooms and bullying **232**.25, 36
chavs, prejudice against **219**.5
cheating in sport, children's views on **198**.38
cheese production using GM organisms **208**.8
chemicals
    impact on wildlife **193**.16-17
    pollution from pharmaceutical waste **218**.38-9
    in tobacco smoke **188**.4, 9-10, 15
chewing and spitting (eating disorders) **249**.8
chewing tobacco **188**.11
chickens *see* hens
child abuse **248**.1-39
    effects **248**.3-5, 26
    faith-based abuse **248**.21-3

getting help **248**.14-15, 26-7
images on the Internet **196**.39
and mental health problems **201**.3
neglect **248**.3, 14-20
physical **248**.3
prevalence **248**.5-6, 7
signs **248**.4, 15, 30
see also corporal punishment; sexual abuse
Child B case **248**.22
child exploitation **202**.1-39
definition **202**.1
reasons for **202**.2
see also child labour; sexual exploitation of
children
Child Exploitation and Online Protection (CEOP)
Centre **248**.35
child labour **202**.1-15**; 229**.15-16
and age of child **202**.3, 16
consumer influence **202**.13-14
definitions **202**.3
domestic labour **202**.12
and education **202**.4-5; **221**.39
elimination **202**.2, 4-5, 7-8, 15
hazards **202**.4, 12
numbers of child labourers **202**.3-4, 6-7
reasons for **202**.5, 12
tobacco pickers **188**.39
Child Labour Index **202**.11
child marriage **202**.19; **244**.15; **248**.24-5
child-on-child abuse **238**.17; **248**.13
child pornography **202**.17-18
legal status, worldwide **246**.9
online **248**.29
child poverty **235**.5, 18-22
and education **235**.21-2
effects **235**.19
quiz **235**.20
statistics **235**.18-19
Child Poverty Act **235**.19
child prostitution **202**.17, 24-6; **246**.27-8, 34-8
Child Protection Delivery Plan (CPDP) **248**.36
child protection
global targets **248**.32-3
legislation **248**.35-6
services **248**.7-8
child safety orders **223**.32
Child Sex Offender Disclosure Scheme **248**.1, 35
child sex tourism **202**.18-19
child sexual exploitation **248**.30, 31
child soldiers **202**.32-9
girls **202**.32, 35-6
numbers **202**.32-3
punishment **202**.34
rehabilitation **202**.36, 37-9
child trafficking **202**.1, 27-31
sex trafficking **246**.35-7
childcare
and children's development **191**.16-17
and fathers **221**.4-5
financial help for young parents **182**.6
gender gap **221**.6
and grandparents **191**.15, 16-17
and welfare reform bill **235**.9

childhood, children's rights to **229**.25
childhood obesity **205**.19; **241**. 19, 35
adoption of obese children **241**.23
bariatric surgery **241**.22
prevention **241**.19-21
childhood problems
and suicide risk **199**.34
childhood survival rate **251**.2
ChildLine **248**.7, 8, 16; **252**.15, 16
number of calls **248**.2
peer support project (CHIPS) **199**.33
and suicide **199**.22, 31, 32, 33
ChildLine in Partnership with Schools (CHIPS)
199.33
children
abuse *see* child abuse
adopted
contact with birth family **247**.16
and education **247**.17
and advertising **207**.35-6, 37, 39; **238**.6-7
aggressive behaviour **224**.22-3
alcohol consumption **194**.1-3, 25-6
influence of household drinking habits **194**.25
of alcoholic parents **194**.27-8
anxiety and phobias **206**.13
attitudes to parents drinking **194**.28
and beauty pageants **238**.28-30
bereavement **192**.4, 5-6, 13-19, 21
facts and figures **192**.12
support **192**.4, 5-6, 10, 17
character skills, importance of **219**.34-5
child-on-child sex attacks **238**.17; **248**.13
and the commercial world **207**.37-9
contact with parents after divorce **191**.11
cricket scheme, improving social well-being
198.3-4
and crime **223**.30-32
sentences for riot crime **223**.29
death, children's understanding of **192**.4, 13, 15,
19
definition, in international conventions **202**.3, 16
development, effect of childcare **191**.16-17
development of character capabilities **191**.6-7
disabled *see* disabled children
discipline *see* discipline
and divorce **191**.1, 9; **244**.36-7
and domestic abuse **224**.24-6, 37
donor conceived **247**.39
eating disorder **249**.3, 7-8, 21, 22
faddy eating **249**.23-4
family background, effect on outcomes **219**.22,
23, 25-6, 27-8, 29-30, 34
financial awareness **250**.21
fluid intake **205**.28
and food additives **205**.14-15
and food advertising **205**.38
and fuel poverty **235**.15-16
and gambling **203**.12-14
problem gambling **203**.20
gender-variant behaviour **225**.23-4
and grief **192**.4, 5-6, 19
and healthy eating
breakfast **205**.8, 9

misleading marketing of children's foods **205**.39

   packed lunches **205**.7, 10

and HIV/AIDS **243**.23-5

   cure of baby born with HIV **243**.37-9

   infection rate reduction **243**.26-7

   transmission from mother **243**.1-2

and homelessness **189**.29-32

information held without parental consent **245**.16

and the Internet **230**.4-5, 25, 33-4; **245**.25-8

LGBT children and schools **225**.5-8

life on the streets **189**.27-8

local authority responsibilities **224**.37

in lone parent families **191**.12

and mental health problems **201**.2-4

missing breakfast **205**.8, 9

missing from care homes **248**.28

money worries **250**.20

National Child Measurement Programme **241**.24

obesity *see* childhood obesity

online privacy awareness **245**.25-6

packed lunches **205**.7, 10

and parental relationships **191**.1

   wellbeing effects of marriage **244**.10

and parental separation **191**.1, 8, 9; **201**.3; **244**.36-7

and passive smoking **188**.5, 11

physical activity guidelines **241**.1, 6, 20

physical inactivity **241**.35

pocket money **250**.39

and poverty *see* child poverty

and prison *see* youth custody

rights of domestic abuse victims **224**.38

and self-harm **199**.17

sexual abuse *see* sexual abuse

sexualisation of young children **221**.9-10; **238**.1-15, 27-36

and smoking **252**.37-9

   passive smoking **188**.5, 11; **252**.38

and social media, parents monitoring **245**.26-7

and social mobility **219**.27

and sport **241**.35-6

as suicide bombers **212**.11-12

time spent with fathers **191**.32

tobacco pickers, health problems **188**.39

toy preferences and gender **221**.7-8

travel to school **200**.1-2, 19-20

undernourishment, developing countries **235**.26-7

and vegetarian diet **214**.28, 36

viewing Internet pornography **196**.38; **238**.3-4; **246**.10-11

and women's attitude to marriage **244**.6-7

and women's careers **183**.21

of working mothers **221**.26

see also boys and young men; girls and young women;

   young people

Children Acts **248**.35

Children and Family Court Advisory and Support Service (Cafcass) **248**.2, 35

children's rights **229**.24-6

   to education **229**.24, 27-8

   UK **229**.29-30

   UN Convention on the Rights of the Child **229**.24-6

China

   child labour **202**.11

   death penalty **229**.37

   economic development **226**.21

   Google withdrawing from China **196**.27-28, 29, 30

   one-child rule **220**.4, 18

   patriotic hacking **196**.34-5

   plastic waste import ban **242**.19

   population trends **220**.8

   poverty rates **235**.23

   privacy rights **245**.4

   straddling bus **200**.29

Chinese medicine, risks **195**.36

CHIPS (ChildLine in Partnership with Schools) **199**.33

chlamydia **237**.20, 22

   rates in young people **252**.2, 3

   testing for **237**.22, 24

chlorinating water, environmental impact **218**.38-9

chocolate, labelling rules **205**.12

Choosing to Die documentary **217**.20

CHP *see* combined heat and power

Christianity **215**.1-2

   and abortion **231**.19

   and Britain **215**.14

   as default religion in Britain **215**.15-16

   and equality legislation **215**.25

   funerals **192**.34

   and the law **215**.26-7

   and pornography **246**.1

   and same-sex marriage **244**.18

   and vegetarianism **214**.6

church attendance **215**.6

Church of England and same-sex marriage **244**.23-4

churches

   and civil partnerships **244**.17

   and marriage **244**.2, 4, 8-9

   and same-sex marriage **244**.23-4, 25

cigar smoking **188**.3

cigarettes

   chemicals in **188**.4, 9-10, 15

   consumption statistics **188**.3

   cost **188**.15, 22

   health warnings on packs ineffective **188**.29

   packaging giving misleading messages **188**.20

   see also smoking

Cinematograph Films (Animals) Act **196**.14

CIRA (Continuity IRA) **212**.14

circuses, use of wild animals **233**.4, 14-15

CITES (Convention on International Trade in Endangered Species) **193**.2

cities *see* cars, congestion; urban areas; urban growth

Citizens Advice and debt help **250**.29-30

citizenship

   citizenship lessons to include financial education **250**.19

   and Muslims **215**.9-10

   tests **220**.30-31; **240**.7

citizenship education **240**.1-2
    Youth Parliament manifesto **240**.38
civil marriage ceremonies **191**.3; **244**.2
civil partnerships **244**.16-18
    dissolution **244**.30-31
    legal equivalence with marriage **225**.35
    for opposite-sex couples **225**.33
    in religious buildings **225**.32; **244**.17
clandestine marriages **244**.9
class *see* social class
classification
    of drugs **186**.32-3; **228**.21, 24, 25
        criticism of **228**.22-3
        designer drugs **228**.32-3
        effect on policing **186**.36-7
        reclassification of cannabis **186**.4-5, 31, 32; **228**.23
    of films **196**.13-16
    of video games **196**.17
climate change **193**.5; **216**.1-39; **218**.19
    adaptation to **216**.28, 29-30
    and British weather **216**.4, 8, 9
    Cancun Agreement **226**.4
    controversies **216**.18-27
    definitions **216**.5
    effects of **216**.4, 6-7, 8, 9, 10-12, 14
    evidence for **216**.3, 5-6, 18-19, 20, 22-4
    and food production **205**.30; **214**.17, 18, 19, 21; **216**.6-7, 10
    and forests **216**.14-15
    and Galapagos Islands **193**.24-5
    international agreements **216**.37-9; **226**.4
    measurement **216**.26-7
    and meat production **214**.17, 18, 19, 21
    mechanisms **216**.2
    and migration **220**.20, 28, 29
    mitigation **216**.7, 28
    political attitudes **216**.25
    predictions **216**.6, 9
    public attitudes **216**.21, 24, 25, 32; **218**.14
    refugees **216**.10-11
    and renewable energy sources
        microgeneration **204**.36
        wind energy **204**.12
    response to **216**.28-39
    scepticism **216**.23-4, 25
    and sea level **216**.9, 16-17, 20-21
    and tourism **222**.22
    UN rainforest protection initiative **218**.20-21
    and water resources **218**.33
    and whales and dolphins **193**.29
    see also energy efficiency; global warming; greenhouse
        gas emissions
climate events of 2010 **216**.13
climate forcing **216**.1
climate justice **218**.4
climate measurement **216**.26-7
climate models **216**.2
climate sensitivity **216**.2
Climbie, Victoria **248**.1
Clinical Commissioning Groups (CGCs) **251**.25, 29, 31

clinical (major) depression **190**.2, 21
cloning *see* animal cloning; human cloning
closed list voting system **240**.29
clothes, energy-harvesting **204**.39
clubs and societies at university **185**.6-7
CO$_2$ *see* carbon dioxide
coach travel, disabled people **197**.12
coal, production trends **204**.1
coastal areas
    effect of climate change **216**.7
    effects of tourism **222**.25
cocoa, labelling rules **205**.12
code layer of privacy **245**.3
coercive control and domestic violence **224**.34-5
coffee
    and hydration **205**.27
    labelling rules **205**.12
Cognitive Behavioural Therapy (CBT); **252**.15, 19
    and phobias **206**.13
    and post traumatic stress disorder, armed forces **213**.34
    and problem gambling **203**.24
    and stress **206**.3, 12
cognitive enhancing drugs **252**.33, 34
cognitive therapy for depression **190**.34
cohabitation
    after relationship breakdown **244**.38-9
    before marriage, and likelihood of divorce **244**.33
    see also common-law marriage
cold weather payments **204**.23
Cole, Cheryl, and cyberbullying **232**.38
Colombia, town banning tourists **222**.32
colourants, food **205**.14-15
colour preferences and gender **221**.7-8
combined heat and power (CHP)
    and fuel cells **204**.38
    microgeneration **204**.35
combined pill **237**.6
commercial radio **210**.3
commercial sexual exploitation of children **202**.16-31
    definition **202**.16
commercialisation, effect on children **207**.38-9
Commission on Funding of Care and Support (Dilnot Report) **239**.20, 22-3
committees, Cabinet **240**.26
Common Agricultural Policy, impact on developing countries **226**.33
common law marriage **244**.8-9
    see also cohabitation
communication
    needs of disabled children **197**.37
    trends **210**.4-5
    see also media; telecommunications; telephones
Communications Data Bill **245**.5-8
    and Internet pornography **246**.8
    objections to **245**.6-7, 8
community heat networks **242**.33
community sentences **223**.20, 23
Community Service Volunteers (CSV) **240**.36
Company magazine, 'pro-skinny' article **249**.27
company boards *see* boardroom positions
company pensions **250**.12

Compassion in Dying information line **217**.37
compensation and the Human Rights Act **229**.5-6
competitive sport in schools **198**.5
complaints process, NHS **251**.26
complementary and alternative medicine (CAM)
    195.1-39
    arguments against **195**.14-15
    definitions **195**.1, 9
    and depression **190**.11
    how it works **195**.2
    need for research **195**.13
    popularity **195**.3
    positive effects **195**.6-7
    reasons for using **195**.5, 6-7
    safety **195**.2
    therapists **195**.1, 3
    types **195**.3
    see also Chinese medicine; herbal medicine;
homeopathy
complementary therapies and depression **190**.11;
    252.19
complicated bereavement **192**.16-17
composting waste **218**.11-12
    gas production **204**.24
comprehensive school pupils, degree performance
    209.12; **219**.32
comprehensive sexuality education **237**.38-9
compressed air energy storage (CAES) **204**.37-8
compulsive exercising **249**.7
compulsive gambling *see* problem gambling
compulsive shopping **207**.6
computed tomography (CT) scanners **251**.2
computer network attacks **196**.34
computers
    late-night use and depression **252**.20
    see also Internet
concentrating solar thermal power (CSP) **204**.3
conception **182**.3-4
    problems *see* infertility
    rate, young people **182**.3; **252**.1, 3
concurrent sentences **223**.19
condoms **182**.19, 20; **237**.2, 3-4, 6, 18-19
    failure **237**.2, 6
    obtaining **237**.3-4, 19
    and the prevention of STIs **237**.18-19
    safe use **237**.2
    use in porn films **246**.5
conflict *see* war
conflict-induced displacement **220**.36-7
conflict minerals **226**.3
congestion, traffic
    London Congestion Charge **200**.17-18
    public attitudes **200**.5-6
Congo
    child soldiers **202**.37-9
    logging industry and wildlife **193**.4
    natural resources and violence **226**.3
Congo River **193**.4
Connelly, Peter (Baby P) **248**.1
consecutive sentences **223**.19
consent, sexual **237**.12-13
conservation *see* endangered species; extinction
constitution, British, and Christianity **215**.14

construction, houses *see* house building
consumer power **207**.3-5
    and ethical consumerism **207**.23-4
consumer rights **207**.12-22
    credit card purchases **207**.12, 18
    online shopping **207**.12, 13
consumer spending *see* spending
consumer trends **207**.1-11
consumerism
    and children **207**.37-9
    problems **207**.2
consumers
    and child labour **202**.13-14
    and child trafficking **202**.30
    disability discrimination **197**.21, 25
    and energy industry **218**.10
    ethical shopping **226**.38
    and food from cloned animals **211**.11, 12, 14
    and GM foods **208**.29-30, 31, 33
    rights *see* consumer rights
    and sustainable development **226**.4
    see also shopping
consumption
    global **193**.3-4
inequality and population growth **220**.11-12, 14, 15
contamination
    of crops by GM crops **208**.24, 27
    see also pollution
contextual targeting **230**.5
Continuity IRA (CIRA) **212**.14
continuous deep sedation **217**.25
contraception **182**.3-4, 19-26; **237**.2, 6-11
    developing countries **220**.16-17
    sources of information **237**.8-9
    and young people **182**.1-2
    see also condoms; family planning; pill,
contraceptive
contraceptive implants **237**.7
contraceptive injections **237**.7
Convention on Action against Trafficking in Human
Beings **246**.31-2
Convention on the Rights of the Child (UN) **202**.2
conversion therapy (homosexuality) **225**.17-18
cookies (Internet) **245**.3, 9-10
cooperation, global **226**.17-19, 22-5
Copenhagen climate change summit **216**.37, 38
copycat suicides and media reporting **199**.36
copyright and the Internet **230**.30, 35-7
coral reefs **193**.5
    economic value **193**.10
    threats to **218**.24
coronary heart disease (CHD) *see* heart disease
coroner **192**.31
Coroners and Justice Act **196**.14
Corporate Social Responsibility **207**.30; **226**.38;
    227.9-10, 12, 18-19
correspondence rights **245**.1
cortisol **206**.30
cosmetic surgery
    desire for **234**.14-15, 19, 33
    Girlguiding UK campaign **234**.34
    regulation **234**.21
cost of living rising faster than earnings **207**.8

costs
  of ageing population **239**.15
  alcohol **194**.35
    minimum pricing **194**.36, 37
  alien invasive species **193**.12
  cannabis **186**.2
  care for the elderly **239**.20-23
  CCTV **245**.28-9
  climate change **216**.4
  communications service **210**.10, 14-15
  domestic violence **224**.27
  drug abuse **228**.1-2, 24
  of eating disorders **249**.
  education **235**.21, 22
  ethical food labelling **207**.29
  of fraud **207**.21-2
  funerals **192**.30-31
  higher education **185**.11, 17
  holidays **222**.5, 6-7
  of mental ill health **201**.1, 5, 23
  of the NHS **251**.8
  of obesity and overweight **241**.3, 18-19
  organic food **207**.30
  of physical inactivity **241**.1-2
  prohibiting couples from divorce and separation
    244.33, 38-9
  smoking **188**.15, 22-3
  student life **185**.11
  university degrees **185**.11, 17
  vegetarian food **214**.12
  wind farms **204**.17-18
  of work-related stress **183**.6-7; **206**.5
cotinine and passive smoking **188**.12
cotton, and child labour **202**.13-14
Council of Europe
  Convention on Action against Trafficking in
  Human Beings **246**.31-2
  convention on domestic violence **224**.32-3
council tax **250**.14
councils see local authorities
counselling
  abortion **231**.24-5, 26-9, 31, 36-7
  couples unable to afford **244**.38
  for depression **190**.34; **239**.31; **252**.15. 19
  and help with stress **206**.2
counter-terrorism **212**.15-25
  legislation **212**.19, 20
  police powers **212**.15-16
  Prevent strategy **212**.17-18
  UK strategy review **212**.21-2, 26, 38-9
Counter Terrorism Act 2008 **212**.19
courts, support for sexual abuse victims **248**.39
cows see cattle
crabs (pubic lice) **237**.21
crash diets **205**.22
creationism teaching at free school **215**.22
credit
  consumer credit levels **207**.16
  credit files **207**.20
  credit ratings **250**.9, 10
  logbook loans **235**.12
  payday loans **235**.11
  see also debt

credit cards
  companies giving incorrect information **207**.17-18
  and consumer rights **207**.12, 18
  fraud **223**.4
credit companies, informing of a death **192**.32
credit crunch see recession
credit unions **235**.11
crime **223**.1-18
  and aggressive behaviour in children **224**.23
  and alcohol **194**.20, 21, 29
  causes of criminal behaviour **223**.11
    rioting **223**.8, 9-10
  and CCTV **245**.29, 30, 31
  committed by children **223**.30-31
  and Communications Data Bill **245**.5
  crime mapping **223**.1-2
  cybercrime **230**.29
  and DNA evidence **245**.14, 15
  and gangs **223**.6-7, 13-15
  HIV transmission as crime **243**.11
  and household insurance **235**.7
  knife crime **223**.5
    prevention **223**.6-7, 16-17, 34
    punishment **223**.21, 25
  levels of crime **223**.2, 3-5
  and licensing hours change **194**.21
  and mental health sufferers **201**.22
  phishing **230**.30
  reporting a crime **223**.12
  riots **223**.8-11
  and sexual exploitation **202**.22
  and slums **235**.37
  victims of see victims of crime
  waste crime **242**.8-9, 10-12
  see also fraud; victims of crime; violent crime;
young offenders
Crime and Courts Bill **248**.34
crime prevention **223**.12-18
  and CCTV **245**.29, 30, 31
  gangs and youth violence **223**.7, 13-15, 35-6
  role of ex-offenders **223**.18
  and schools **223**.16-17
Criminal Justice Act and hate crime **225**.31
Criminal Justice and Immigration Act **196**.14
  and pornography **246**.8
Criminal Justice and Police Act, and prostitution
  246.18
criminal justice system **223**.19-39
  and children **223**.29, 30-32
  and ethnic minorities **236**.9, 10
  gang injunctions **223**.35-6
  reforms **223**.24-5
  restorative justice **223**.28-9
  sentencing **223**.19-22, 23, 33
  see also prison
criminal responsibility, age of **223**.30
  reasons for raising **223**.31-2
criminalisation of demand for prostitution **246**.20
  impact on sex trafficking **246**.33
criminalisation of homosexuality, globally **225**.39
criminals
  and the Human Rights Act **229**.5, 6
  see also prisoners

crop biotechnology *see* genetically modified (GM) crops

cross-contamination, GM crops **208**.24, 26

crossdressers **225**.19

crowdsourcing CCTV monitoring **245**.30

cruise ships, impact on environment **222**.25

cryopreservation *see* freezing

crystal meth (methamphetamine) **228**.23

CSE (comprehensive sexuality education) **237**.38-9

CSP (concentrating solar thermal power) **204**.3

CSS (carbon capture and storage) **204**.27

CSV (Community Service Volunteers) **240**.36

cultural identity
    British *see* British identity

cultural traditions and death **192**.29, 34-6

culture
    and age discrimination **239**.6-7
    and body image **234**.3
    British **240**.3, 14
    and fatherhood **191**.33
    effect of tourism **222**.22, 29, 30

Cura (website for carers) **239**.38

curriculum
    and faith schools **215**.19
    reform **209**.5

custody *see* prison; youth custody

customer service lines **207**.14
    credit card companies **207**.17-18

customs regulations on indecent articles **196**.23

cutting (self-harm)
    emergency treatment **199**.13-14
    safety measures **199**.7

CVD *see* cardiovascular disease

cyber stalking **230**.23

cyberbullying **230**.23; **232**.2, 25-39
    dealing with **232**.3, 26, 29, 39
    effects **232**.25, 26
    forms **232**.25
    prevalence **232**.30, 31
    preventing **230**.28; **232**.26-7, 28
    reasons for **232**.25-6
    reporting **232**.29
    at work **227**.38

cybercrime **230**.29

cycling **200**.21
    cycles sharing roads with cars **200**.18
    impact of traffic **200**.16
    to school **200**.1-2

cyclothymia **190**.9; **201**.15

D

D&E (surgical dilation and evacuation) **231**.7

dairy farming, mega-dairies **233**.9-10

dairy foods *see* milk; milk products

dancing, health benefits for older people **241**.33-4

Dangerous Dogs Act **233**.4, 12-13

dark tourism **222**.16

Data Communications Bill *see* Communications Data Bill

Data Protection Act **245**.11

data protection laws, worldwide **245**.4

date labels on food packaging **242**.14, 15

date rape drugs **194**.8-10

dead zones, oceans **218**.24-5

deafness **239**.25

death penalty **223**.37-9; **229**.37-8
    and European Court of Human Rights **229**.39

deaths
    AIDS-related **243**.6, 26, 27
    alcohol-related **194**.13
    in Armed Forces **213**.9
    of children **192**.20-23
    children's understanding of death **192**.4, 13, 15, 19
    discussing own wishes about dying **192**.8, 24
    drug-related **228**.2, 13
    earlier death of mental health sufferers **201**.26
    from eating disorders **249**.5, 16
    funerals **192**.30-31, 34-7
    older people, risk increased by loneliness **239**.36-7
    practical matters **192**.24, 29-33
    registering **192**.29-30
    see also bereavement; euthanasia; mortality

Debenhams, using disabled model **197**.10

DeBique, Tilern **213**.13-14

debt
    advice **250**.29-30, 31, 33, 37-8
    buying on credit **207**.6, 16
    developing world **226**.5-6
    health impacts **250**.29, 33
    levels of debt **250**.5, 11, 32
    students **185**.12-13, 17; **209**.31-2

debt cancellation, developing countries **226**.5-6

debt crisis **226**.5

Declaration of Internet Freedom **230**.37

decriminalisation
    of drugs possession **228**.34
    of prostitution **246**.20

default retirement age **183**.14-15

defence
    budget cuts **213**.17-19, 20-21, 22-3, 28
    see also Armed Forces

deforestation
    and cattle ranching **193**.14
    dryland forests **218**.21
    and palm oil industry **193**.14
    rainforest protection programme **218**.20-21

degrees, university
    costs **185**.11, 17
    courses **185**.5-6
    and earnings **185**.21, 32-4
    and students' school background **209**.12; **219**.32

dementia **239**.4, 5, 28-9
    and depression **201**.12-13
    worries about **239**.30
    in younger people **201**.10-11
    see also Alzheimer's disease

dementia services **201**.5, 10-11

democracy
    and Islam **215**.10
    see also electoral systems

demographic transition **220**.3

demographics *see* population; population growth
demonstrations via the Internet **196**.32
Denmark, energy from waste **242**.33
dental dams **237**.18-19
Department of Health **251**.30
dependency, on alcohol **194**.6, 15
deportation of non-nationals, and Human Rights
    Act **229**.4-5
depressant drugs (downers) **228**.3
    see also cannabis; heroin; solvents
depression **190**.1-39; **239**.24-5
    anti-depressant drugs *see* anti-depressant drugs
    and cannabis use **186**.10
    causes of **190**.2-3, 4, 5
    in children and young people **252**.18-19
    and complementary therapies **190**.11
    definitions **190**.21-2
    and dementia **201**.12-13; **239**.32
    and desire for success **190**.13
    diagnosis
        bipolar disorder **190**.8
        GPs difficulty diagnosing depression **190**.31
        teenage depression **190**.25-6
    and eating disorders **249**.3
    and exercise **190**.3, 38
    and fast food **252**.24
    genetic factors **190**.2, 4, 11, 12-13
    and HIV diagnosis **243**.13, 31
    and late night screen use **252**.20
    manic depression *see* bipolar affective disorder
    and meditation **190**.34-6; **195**.15
    and men **190**.18-19
    and mortality **190**.20
    and older people **239**.31-2
        living with HIV **243**.31
    and physical illness **190**.3, 5
    post-natal **190**.2, 14-17, 21-2
    prevalence of **190**.22-3, 30
    and redundancy **183**.11
    statistics **190**.7, 27, 30
    students **185**.8
    and suicide **190**.21, 23-4
        young people **190**.26-7
    symptoms **190**.1-2; 21, 22; **199**.29; **239**.31
        bipolar disorder **190**.8-9, 21
        post-natal depression **190**.14
        seasonal affective disorder **190**.6
        young people **190**.26
    treatments **190**.31-9; **239**.31
        drugs **190**.10-11, 26, 32-3
        see also anti-depressant drugs
        manic depression **190**.10-11
        psychotherapy **190**.5, 11, 34, 37
        Seasonal Affective Disorder **190**.6-7
        self-help **190**.38-9; **239**.31-2
        young people **190**.25
    types of **190**.2, 21-2
    unipolar (endogenous) **190**.10
    young people **190**.25-30; **252**.18-19
        unemployed **252**.21
    see also bipolar affective disorder, (manic
depression);
        seasonal affective disorder (SAD)

desertion as grounds for divorce **244**.30, 31
designer drugs, control of **228**.32-3
desoxypipradol **228**.25, 37
determinate sentences **223**.19-20
detox diets **205**.22
developed countries, impact of globalisation
    226.24-5
developing countries
    age structures **220**.8
    aid to *see* aid
    biofuels causing food shortages **204**.33-4
    child labour **202**.9-12
    and climate change **216**.11
    and contraception **220**.16-17
    dangers of homeopathy **195**.30-31
    debt **226**.5-6
    definition **226**.30
    education **209**.8; **229**.27-8
    fertility rates **220**.2, 3, 4, 12, 13
    and free trade **226**.32, 33-4
    gender inequality **221**.1-2, 35
    girls' education **221**.35, 38-9; **229**.27-8
    and globalisation **226**.3-4
    and GM crops **208**.10
    and ICT **230**.7
    loans for small businesses **235**.33-5
    and population growth **220**.2, 4, 5-7
    and poverty **235**.23-39
    poverty reduction strategies **235**.24
    remittances from migrant workers **220**.35
    and renewable energy **204**.2
    slum tourism **222**.16, 33-4
    and transport **200**.13
    UK trade initiatives **226**.28
    World Bank support **226**.9-10
    and World Trade Organization **226**.8
    see also Millennium Development Development
        Goals
development-induced displacement **220**.37
Devil's in Your Details campaign **245**.22
devolved government **240**.27-8
diabetes **239**.25; **241**.3
    and bulimia (diabulimia) **249**.11
    in children and young people **252**.8
    and meat consumption **214**.35
    prevalence **241**.3, 9
diet
    children **252**.29
    healthy *see* healthy eating
    importance of breakfast **205**.8-9
    macrobiotic **195**.4-5
    and mental health **190**.3; **252**.24, 25
    and overweight **241**.15-16
    and stress **206**.33
    UK population **205**.1, 17
    young people **252**.4
    see also dieting; eating disorders; food and
        nutrition; healthy eating; veganism; vegetarianism
diet industry **234**.7-8
dietary obsession (orthorexia nervosa) **249**.8
dietary supplements **205**.4
    and vegetarian diet **214**.10, 29
dieting **205**.22-3

and body image **234**.12
digital dating abuse **224**.20
digital fluency **230**.10-12
digital footprints **230**.31-2
digital literacy **230**.13
digital natives **230**.8-9
Dignity in Dying **217**.38
    criticism of assisted suicide policy **217**.26
        dilation and evacuation (abortion) **231**.7
diplomas, gender-stereotypical choices **221**.28
direct discrimination
    against Gypsies and Travellers **236**.22
    racial **236**.1-2
    sexual orientation **225**.28
directors, company *see* boardroom positions
disability
    and abortion **231**.20
    acceptable language **197**.27
    benefits **197**.31-4
    definitions **197**.1-2
    discrimination **197**.20-23
        in healthcare **197**.30-31, 38-9
        workplace **197**.20-21
        see also Disability Discrimination Act
    and employment **197**.20-21, 24-5, 26-7
    hidden disabilities **197**.8
    learning disabilities **197**.6-7
    and mental health, young people **201**.3
    and older people **239**.4
    physical disabilities **197**.3-5
    and poverty **197**.35
    and transport **197**.11-12, 23
    see also disabled children; disabled people
Disability Discrimination Act **197**.8-9, 24-5
    and workplace stress **206**.28
Disability Living Allowance **197**.31-4
disability rights
    access to goods and services **197**.21, 25
    education **197**.22-3
    housing **197**.21-2
    transport **197**.11-12, 23
    at work **197**.20-21, 24-5, 26-7
Disability Symbol **197**.26-7
disabled children
    learning disabilities **197**.14-15
    needs **197**.36-7
    physical disabilities **197**.3-5
    siblings of disabled children **197**.18-19
disabled people
    and assisted suicide **199**.39; **217**.19, 21
    benefit cuts **229**.32
    discrimination **197**.20-23, 30-31, 38-9
      see also Disability discrimination Act
    and domestic abuse **224**.4
    and employment **197**.20-21, 24-5, 26-7
    in low-income households **235**.5, 7
    model used in advertising campaign **197**.10
    and sport **198**.18, 20-21
    and transport **197**.11-12, 23
    see also disability; learning disabilities
disablism *see* discrimination, disabled people
disaster-induced displacement **220**.37
disaster tourism **222**.16
discipline, role of fathers **191**.31-2

DISCO, EU biofuels project **204**.32
discrimination
    anti-discrimination legislation **183**.13; **221**.3, 36
        and workplace stress **206**.28-9
    and child trafficking **202**.28
    against Christians **215**.25
    definition **221**.3
    disabled people **197**.20-23
        in healthcare **197**.30-31, 38-9
        at work **197**.20-21
        see also Disability Discrimination Act
    gender discrimination at work **221**.18, 23-4
        see also gender pay gap
    against HIV sufferers **243**.15, 16-17
    against Muslims **215**.30, 31-2
    racial *see* racial discrimination
    religious **215**.23-4; 30; 31-2
        and same-sex marriage views **244**.24, 25
    sexual orientation **225**.9-10, 28-9
        and religious beliefs **225**.35
    in the workplace **197**.20-21; **215**.23-4; **221**.18, 23-4
    see also prejudice; racism; sex discrimination
disease
    resistance, GM crops **208**.1, 29
    stem cell treatment **211**.30, 36-7, 38-9
disordered eating **249**.10
displaced people *see* refugees
dispute settlement, World Trade Organization **226**.8
distraction techniques, self-harmers **199**.5-6, 8
diuretics as banned substances in sport **198**.29
divorce **244**.30-39
    and alcohol consumption **244**.32
    benefits **244**.37
    divorce rate **244**.31
    and children **191**.1, 9
    and children's mental health **201**.3
    grounds for **244**.30
    risk factors **244**.32-3
    statistics **191**.1, 8
DNA **208**.7; **211**.3; **245**.14
    damage by cannabis use **186**.14
DNA database **245**.14-15
Do Not Attempt Resuscitation (DNAR) order **217**.3, 14
docking dogs' tails **233**.6
doctors
    and abortion **231**.2, 25, 28, 29, 32-3
    asking about patient's alcohol consumption **194**.33, 37-8
    and assisted suicide **217**.4, 8, 11, 22, 24-5, 31
    impact of legalizing assisted dying **217**.4, 8, 11, 31
    see also GPs (general practitioners); physician-assisted suicide (PAS)
doctrine of double effect **217**.5, 14
DofE (Duke of Edinburgh's) Award **240**.37
Dog Control Bill **233**.4
doggy box scheme, restaurants **242**.39
dogs
    and animal rights **233**.4
    Dangerous Dogs Act **233**.4, 12-13
    tail docking **233**.6

Dolly the sheep **211**.7, 8
dolphins
    dolphin-watching holidays **222**.26
    impact of climate change **193**.29
    rights **233**.20
domestic abuse **224**.1-39
    children **189**.27
    costs **224**.27
    definitions **224**.1, 34-7
    excuses for **224**.1-2
    help for perpetrators **224**.39
    help for victims **224**.38
    impact on children **224**.24-6, 37
    lesbian, gay ,bisexual and transgender
relationships **224**.5, 12-13
    male victims **224**.5, 9-10, 11
    and mental health of children **201**.3
    myths **224**.6-7
    personal stories **224**.8, 21, 26
    prevalence of **224**.28
    prevention strategy **224**.28-31
    signs of abuse
        in children **224**.24, 25
        in teenagers **224**.16-17
    statistics **224**.11
    staying with an abusive partner **224**.6
    support for victims **224**.38
    and young people **224**.4, 16-26
domestic waste see household waste
domestic workers
    children **202**.12
    and human trafficking **229**.18
donor insemination **247**.7-8
    giving information to children **247**.39
'don't ask don't tell' policy, US military **225**.38-9
doping see drugs in sport
Dove, self-esteem campaign **234**.33
downers see depressant drugs
downshifting **183**.18
drag queens/kings **225**.19
Drax power plant, biomass fuel **204**.5, 7
drink-driving **194**.31
    reducing alcohol limit **194**.32
drink spiking **194**.8-10
drinking water access **218**.31-3, 36
driving
    and alcohol see drink-driving
    and cannabis use **186**.10
    dementia sufferers **201**.11
    and disabled people **197**.11
    motorway phobia **200**.4
drought **218**.23
drug abuse **228**.1-39
    and beggars **189**.35-6
    costs **228**.1-2, 24
    deaths from **228**.2, 13; **252**.32
    declining **228**.35
    drug education campaign **228**.10-11
    effects **228**.12-13
    and HIV **243**.7
    and homeless people **189**.10, 13, 35-6
    ketamine **228**.5
    legal highs **228**.1, 36-8; **252**.32

needle sharing and HIV transmission **243**.1
signs of **228**.14-15
statistics **228**.1, 13, 35
smart drugs **252**.33, 34
students **185**.8, 9
treatment **228**.16-18
trends **228**.1
types of drugs **228**.3-4
worldwide **186**.18-21
young people **252**.1, 31, 32, 35
see also cannabis
drug development and animal experiments see
animal experiments
drug gangs, targeted by National Crime Agency
223.22
drug overdoses, emergency treatment **199**.14;
228.2
drug policy **228**.24-7
    and designer drugs **228**.32-3
    need for review **228**.39
    see also classification of drugs
drug testing
    in sport **198**.27, 28
        punishment for missing tests **198**.39
drug treatments
    for depression **190**.32-3
        for bipolar disorder **190**.10-11
        as cause of depression **190**.3; **239**.32
        and teenage depression **190**.26
        see also anti-depressants for gambling
            addiction **203**.27
drugs
    animal research in drug development **233**.30-33
    assessment of drug harms **186**.33
    for assisted dying, availability **217**.34
    cannabis see cannabis
    classification **228**.21, 24, 25
        cannabis **186**.4-5, 31, 32-3; 23
        criticism of **228**.22-3
    date rape drugs **194**.8-10
    decriminalisation campaign **228**.34
    definition **228**.21
    effects **228**.4, 12-20
        cannabis **186**.1-29
    fertility drugs **247**.8-9
    global illicit drugs problem **186**.20-21
    government policies **186**.35-6; **228**.24-7
    and the law **228**.21-39; **228**.13, 21-39
    and politics **186**.34-6
    types **228**.3-4
    see also drug abuse; medicines
drugs in sport **198**.27-39
    anabolic steroids **198**.29-30
    analgesics **198**.28-9
    arguments for and against **198**.33-7
    dangers **198**.34
    diuretics **198**.29
    drug testing **198**.27, 28, 39
    history of **198**.32
    hormones **198**.29-30
    reasons for taking drugs **198**.28, 32
    stimulants **198**.29
    therapeutic use exemption **198**.28

dryland forests **218**.21
dual diagnosis **201**.9, 17
  homeless people **189**.10-11
Duke of Edinburgh's Award **240**.37
dumping (trade) **226**.30, 32
dumping of waste, illegal **242**.8-9, 10, 12
dysthymia **190**.10, 21, 23

E

e-bullying *see* cyberbullying
e-cigarettes **188**.21
E-number food additives **205**.14
EAPs (Employment Assistance Programmes) **206**.27
early marriage **202**.19
early onset dementia **201**.10-11
early years education *see* foundation stage
education
earnings
  attitudes to wage levels **219**.15
  footballers **198**.11-12
  gender gap *see* gender pay gap
  graduates **183**.34; **185**.32-4
    and university status **185**.21
  minimum wage, young workers **183**.28
  see also incomes; salaries; wages
Eastern European migrants, UK **220**.24-5
  as victims of racism **236**.32
eating disorders **249**.1-39
  causes **249**.2-3, 17-18, 21, 32
  children **249**.3, 7-8, 21, 22
  as effect of child abuse **248**.4-5
  effects **249**.5, 14
  getting help **249**.4, 5, 20, 21, 34
  and the media **249**.15, 25-31
  prevalence **249**.4, 15-16
  self-help **249**.3-4
  students **185**.8
  treatments **249**.32-9
  see also anorexia nervosa; bulimia nervosa;
obesity
eating habits
  students **209**.32, 33
  see also diet; healthy eating
ECO (Energy Company Obligation) **253**.35
eco-housing **216**.29-30
eco-lodges **222**.24
eco-towns **253**.36
Ecominds **241**.12
economic (financial) abuse **224**.3
economic growth
  Brazil **226**.20-21
  China **226**.21
  and globalisation **226**.3-4
  and higher education **183**.34
  impact of climate change **216**.11-12
  impact of population growth **220**.7
  need for international cooperation **226**.17-19
  role of business **227**.14
economy
  global, and biodiversity **193**.10-12

recession *see* recession
  and tobacco **188**.22-3
  and tourism **222**.28, 30
    Britain **222**.4-5
ecosystems
  biodiversity **218**.18
  impact of climate change **216**.6
ecotourism **222**.8-9, 22-3, 24-5, 27-8
ecstasy (MDMA), signs of use **228**.14
ECT (electro-convulsive therapy) **190**.11
ectopic pregnancy risk in IVF **247**.7
EDCs (endocrine disrupting chemicals) **193**.16-17
Editor's Code (Press Complaints Commission)
    210.27-8
EDNOS (eating disorder not otherwise specified)
    249.7
education **209**.1-39
  and adopted children **247**.17
  and alcohol **194**.20
  and body image **234**.11, 21, 29-30
  effects of cannabis use **186**.9-10
  and child labour **202**.4-5, 14
  and child poverty **235**.21-2
  and child trafficking **202**.28
  children's rights **229**.24-5
  citizenship **240**.1-2, 38
  in developing countries **209**.8; **229**.27-8
  and disabled children **197**.14-15, 22-3, 37
  on drugs, campaign for **228**.10-11
  early years, and social mobility **219**.17-18, 34-5
  and ethnic minorities **236**.10
  faith-based schools **215**.17-22
  financial **250**.17, 19, 21
  girls
    barriers to education **221**.35, 38-9
    and population control **220**.7
  global gender inequality **221**.1, 35
  higher education *see* higher education;
universities
  about HIV/AIDS **243**.10-11
  ICT skills **230**.13
  international comparisons **183**.34
  and learning disabilities **197**.14-15
  Millennium Development Goals **218**.39; **229**.27-8
  about online privacy **245**.26
  about pornography **246**.12-14
  and poverty **202**.4; **235**.21-2
  and racism **236**.15, 16
  and relationship abuse **224**.17
  and sexualisation of children **238**.4, 11, 14
  single-sex schools **221**.30-32
  and social mobility **219**.17-18, 22, 23, 25-6, 27-8, 34-5
  special educational needs (SEN) **197**.14-15, 23
  and teenage pregnancy **182**.31
  see also educational achievement; schools; sex
education; students; teachers; universities
Education and Inspection Act 2006 **225**.7
educational achievement
  and bullying **232**.8
  and child poverty **235**.21
  degree level, and school background **209**.12; **219**.32

and environmental behaviour **218**.9

and importance of British identity **240**.20

on same-sex marriage **244**.21, 24

and parental support **219**.33

and socio-economic background **209**.13-14; **219**.22, 23, 25-6, 27-8, 29-30, 34

standards improving **209**.7-10

statistics **235**.6

terrorist suspects **212**.9

white British pupils, effect of social class **219**.29-30

see also exam results

Educational Maintenance Allowance (EMA) **182**.6; **209**.17, 18

EEA (European Environment Agency) **200**.22

egg donation for research cloning **211**.30

eggs and vegetarian diets **214**.2

Egypt, girls' education **229**.27-8

Ehrlich, Paul **220**.11

elderly people *see* older people

electoral systems **240**.29

electric buses **200**.28-9

electric cars **200**.26, 27; **204**.7

electricity markets, Europe **204**.11-12

electro-convulsive therapy (ECT) **190**.11

electronic cigarettes **188**.21

electronic waste **242**.20-21

EU exports **242**.19

illegal trade **218**.15-16

elephants, as endangered species **193**.2, 19

elevated water storage **204**.38

Elizabeth II (Queen) **240**.22-3

EMA (Educational Maintenance Allowance) **182**.6; **209**.17, 18

email

and bullying **232**.25

security **232**.27

support for anxiety sufferers **252**.14-15

embedded water **218**.35

embryo cloning *see* human reproductive cloning

embryo splitting **211**.24

embryonic stem cells **211**.28, 29-30, 35-6

see also therapeutic cloning

embryos

moral status **211**.31, 34

and stem cell research **211**.31-2

EMDR (Eye Movement Desensitizing and Reprocessing) **213**.34

emergency contraception **182**.5; **237**.2

emergency treatment

drug abuse **228**.2

drug overdose **199**.14

self-harmers **199**.13-14

emissions

reduction **200**.15

standards **200**.15

transport **200**.14, 22

see also greenhouse gas emissions

Emissions Trading Scheme and airlines **222**.14-15

emotional abuse **224**.1, 3

and children's mental health **201**.3

emotional distress

and eating disorders **249**.3

and self-harm **199**.2

emotional effects of child abuse **248**.3, 4, 17, 26

emotional extremes and self-harm **199**.10-11

emotional health

and homelessness **189**.9

see also mental health

emotional neglect **248**.3

emotional signs of stress **206**.9, 19

employees, gay and lesbian **225**.9

employers

involvement in schools **219**.26

links with universities **209**.29

potential use of social networks data **245**.23-4

views on qualifications **209**.3

employment

and age discrimination **239**.6, 12-13

black students' employment prospects **236**.19-20

difficulty finding jobs **235**.6

Disability Symbol **197**.26-7

of disabled people **197**.20-21, 24-5, 26-7

employment status and smoking **188**.2

ethnic pay gap **236**.18

ethnic minorities **236**.10-11

ex-offenders **223**.26-7

ex-service personnel **213**.32

and free trade **226**.13-14

and gender **221**.1-2, 18, 19, 27-9, 37

and globalisation **226**.22

graduates **185**.30, 31-2, 36-7

value of extra-curricula interests **185**.7

and homelessness **189**.33

international labour standards **229**.14-16

living wage for garment workers **229**.13

and mental health sufferers **201**.11, 22-3, 27

Millennium Development Goal **235**.26

migrant workers *see* migrant workers

money worries, impact on work **250**.33

National Insurance **250**.15

and obesity **205**.20

and online reputation **230**.32

past retirement age **239**.16, 18

and population growth **220**.6

by private sector businesses **227**.4

and race discrimination **236**.20

rights

awareness of **183**.10

disability rights **197**.20-21, 24-5, 26-7

international standards **229**.14-16

maternity rights **191**.37-8

parental leave **191**.34 39

paternity rights **191**.34-5, 39

and religious belief **215**.23-4

students **250**.24

tourism industry **222**.21, 30

Britain **222**.4

youth training scheme **222**.31

workplace pensions **250**.12

see also hours of work; jobs; part-time jobs; unemployment; women in the workforce; work-life balance; workplace bullying; workplace stress

Employment Assistance Programmes (EAPs) **206**.27

empty forest syndrome **193**.20

empty homes **253**.18, 32-5

empty nest syndrome **191**.29
empty shops **207**.9
enacted stigma about HIV **243**.16
End Child Exploitation campaign **202**.2
End of Life Assistance (Scotland) Bill **217**.30
end-of-life care, Liverpool Care Pathway **251**.15
end-of-life rights information line **217**.37
End Violence Against Women (EVAW) Coalitition **224**.31
endangered species **193**.1-2
    butterflies **193**.36
    conservation work by zoos **233**.25, 26
    elephants **193**.19
    fish **193**.30
    invertebrates **193**.26
    pollinating insects **193**.27-8
    primates **193**.22-3
    tigers **193**.18
    in the UK **193**.31-2, 35, 36
    whales and dolphins **193**.29
    wildlife tourism **222**.26
    see also extinction; wildlife
endocrine disrupting chemicals **193**.16-17
endogenous (unipolar) depression **190**.10, 22-3
endometriosis **247**.2
energy **204**.1-39
    and consumer choice **218**.10
    energy companies, human rights considerations **229**.9
    energy policies
        EU **204**.30-31
        UK **204**.7-8, 28-9
    industry trends **204**.1
    microgeneration **204**.35
    renewable *see* renewable energy
    saving through recycling **242**.24
    storage **204**.37
    from waste **242**.32-3, 37
    see also fuel poverty
Energy Company Obligation (ECO) **253**.35
energy consumption **204**.1
energy efficiency
    costs **253**.35
    in the home **235**.16
    of housing stock **253**.1
    and sustainable housing **253**.37
    see also renewable energy
England
    abortion law **231**.3
    biodiversity loss **193**.31-2
    devolution **240**.28
    health and physical activity **241**.1-4
    homelessness statistics **189**.3
    rough sleepers **189**.16
    teenage pregnancy **182**.2, 7, 10
English people and national identity **240**.6, 8, 12, 18
entertainment industry and ethnic minorities **236**.12
entrepreneurship
    aspirations **183**.7; **227**.6
    challenges to **227**.8
    developing countries **235**.33-5
    government initiative **227**.7
Entry to Employment (e2e) **183**.29

environment
    and agriculture **214**.16, 17,18-19, 21, 22, 23, 26
    definition **218**.1
    environmental causes of migration **220**.20, 38, 39
    and food production **205**.30, 31-2
        organic farming **205**.34, 35
    sustainable housing **253**.36, 37
    and vegetarian food production **214**.26
    and vegetarianism **214**.15-27
    see also environmental impact; sustainable
        development; wildlife
environmental governance, international **193**.12
environmental impact
    biodegradable products **218**.37
    biofuels **204**.33-4
    chemical pollutants **218**.38-9
    free trade **226**.32
    GM crops **208**.20-21, 22, 29
    globalisation **226**.4
    meat production **214**.18-19, 20-21; 23
    non-agricultural market access (NAMA) **226**.15-16
    plastic bags **242**.26-7
    population growth **218**.26-7, 28; **220**.4, 6-7, 14
    tourism **222**.21, 22, 25, 27, 28, 29
    transport **200**.1, 14-15, 16, 22, 24-5
        reducing **200**.15, 19-20, 25
    waste incineration **242**.34
environmental justice **218**.3-4
environmental retailing **207**.34
environmental sustainability *see* sustainability
environmental tobacco smoke *see* passive smoking
environmental tourism *see* ecotourism
epilepsy
    in children and young people **252**.8
    and exercise **198**.23
Equal Love campaign **225**.33
equal pay *see* gender pay gap
Equal Pay Act **221**.35-6
equality
    and faith schools **215**.18-19, 20
    legislation and religious belief **215**.25
Equality Act 2010 **183**.13; **221**.3, 36
    and LGBT people in schools **225**.6
    and mental health **201**.31
Equality and Human Rights Commission **197**.25; **229**.34
equality at work **183**.12, 26-7
equity loans **253**.7-8, 9
Essentials magazine, diversity award **234**.38
ethical consumerism **202**.13; **207**.23-39; **226**.38
    and child labour **202**.13-14
    statistics **207**.24
ethical food, labelling costs **207**.29
ethical investment and tax compliance **227**.33
ethical tourism *see* ecotourism; responsible travel;
sustainable tourism
ethical trade *see* fair trade
Ethical Trading Initiative (ETI) **226**.27
ethical volunteering **222**.38-9
ethics
    and abortion **231**.16-29
    and animal cloning **211**.10

and biotechnology **211**.6
of euthanasia and assisted suicide **217**.1-23
of human cloning **211**.8-9, 26-7
and stem cell research **211**.30-31, 34
and tourism industry **222**.31-2
Ethiopia, girls' education and child marriage **244**.15
ethnic diversity, Britain **240**.15-16
ethnic equality, public opinion **229**.12
ethnic minorities
    and British identity **240**.18-20
    and employment **236**.10-11, 20
    life in Britain **236**.6-12
    and low income households **235**.7-8
    and mental health problems **201**.2
    women and poverty **221**.34
    see also Asian people; black people; employment and
        racism; racism
ethnic origin
    British population **240**.15-16
    poverty and educational achievement **209**.13-14
    rough sleepers **189**.17
ethnic pay gap **236**.18
ethnic stereotypes
    reducing through tourism **222**.30
Etz Chaim Jewish school **215**.21-2
Europe
    attitudes to biotechnology **211**.5-6
    child soldiers **202**.33
    domestic violence treaty **224**.32-3
    and LGBT equality **225**.39
    press freedom **196**.2
    see also European Union
European Convention on Human Rights **229**.1, 8, 36
    Article 8 on privacy **245**.1
European Court of Human Rights
    death penalty cases **229**.39
    margin of appreciation **229**.6
European Environment Agency (EEA) **200**.22
European Union
    AIDS strategy support **243**.29
    animal welfare legislation **233**.2
    complementary medicine research **195**.16
    elderly people
        poverty risk **239**.17, 18
        quality of life **239**.8-9
    electricity markets **204**.11-12
    energy scenarios **204**.30-31
    environmental policy **218**.7-8
    and GM crops **208**.11, 12
    immigration decline **220**.31
    and LGBT equality **225**.11-13
    migration to UK **220**.24-5
    poverty of elderly people **239**.17, 18
    transport policies **200**.15
    waste exports **242**.18-19
    wind energy **204**.11
    UK relationship **240**.21-2
    Youth Parliament manifesto **240**.39
euthanasia **217**.1-39
    arguments against **217**.2, 3-4, 5-6, 7-8
    arguments for **217**.3, 9-10, 11-12
    definitions **217**.1, 5

doctors' opposition to **217**.22
involuntary 5, 32
and the law **217**.1, 24-39
occurrence in UK **217**.24-5
in other countries **217**.2
public attitudes to **217**.23, 34
see also advance directives; assisted suicide; physician
    assisted suicide (PAS)
eutrophication threat to ocean life **218**.24-5
EVAW (End Violence Against Women) Coalition
    224.31
Everyday Champions Academy **215**.22
evidence
    obtained under torture **229**.21-2
    secret intelligence to be allowed in court **223**.21-2
Evolve Sport **241**.35
ex-offenders
    and employment **223**.26-7
    role in cutting youth crime **223**.18
ex-service personnel **213**.31-9
    finding employment **213**.32
    homelessness **189**.6; **213**.35
    mental health **213**.33-4
    as mentors to young people **213**.32
    in prison **213**.4, 36, 37-9
exams
    A-levels as predictor of degree performance
        209.12; **219**.32
    and pressure on schools **209**.4
    reform **209**.6
    standards **209**.7-10
    and stress **252**.16-17
    use of smart drugs **252**.33, 34
    see also A-levels; GCSEs
exercise
    children **241**.20, 35-6
        lack of exercise **241**.35
    compulsive **249**.7
    dancing, health benefits for older people **241**.33-4
    and depression **190**.3, 7, 38
    fitness training tips **241**.25-6
    and fluid intake **205**.28
    and health **241**.1-6, 8, 9, 32, 33-4
    and health problems **198**.23
    lack of *see* inactivity
    low volume high-intensity training **241**.27-8
    and mental health **190**.3, 38; **241**.4; **252**.26
    motivation for **241**.26, 31
    and obesity **241**.16
    Olympic legacy **241**.9, 10
    and pregnancy **182**.15
    recommended amounts **241**.1, 6, 25
    running **241**.31, 32, 38-9
    and stress reduction **206**.33, 37
    and vegetarian diet **214**.29
    women's reluctance to exercise outdoors **241**.11-12
    Zombies, Run! fitness app **241**.38-9
    see also sport
exhaust gases *see* emissions, transport

exotic species
    in the wild, Britain **193**.39
    trade in **193**.20-21
Expand SkillForce Core Programme **213**.32
expression, freedom of *see* freedom of expression
Extended Determinate Sentence **223**.21
extended licence period **223**.21
extra-marital sex and risk of heart attack **244**.33
extremism
    in schools **212**.12
    at universities **212**.13-14
Eye Movement Desensitization and Reprocessing (EMDR) **213**.34

F

Facebook
    addiction to **230**.15
    censorship of sexual content **196**.37
    children's use of **245**.25
    potential for data mining **245**.23-4
    and privacy **210**.33-4
    reporting inappropriate content **232**.35
    usage trends **245**.24
factory farming **233**.3, 7-8
Faculty of Homeopathy **195**.22
faddy eating **249**.23-4
fairness, children's rights to **229**.26
fairness complaints against broadcasters **196**.20
Fairtrade **207**.32, 33; **226**.30, 31, 36-7
    ineffectiveness **207**.33
Fairtrade Foundation **226**.27
faith *see* religion
faith-based child abuse **248**.21-3
faith-based medicine, difficulty of regulating **195**.36
faith healing **195**.5
faith schools **209**.22-3, 24; **215**.17-20
    and free schools programme **215**.21-2
fallopian tube damage and infertility **247**.2
families
    of cannabis users **186**.23-5
    changing family patterns **191**.1-4
    of disabled young people **197**.18-19
    of drug users **186**.23-5
    family breakdown
        and children's wellbeing **191**.9; **244**.36
        and paternal contact **191**.11
        and youth homelessness **189**.21, 26, 27
        see also divorce
    family structure, effect on children's character **191**.6
    financial difficulties **250**.5
    and gambling **203**.33
    and homelessness **189**.29-32
    income, and educational attainment **219**.22, 23, 25-6, 27-8, 29-30, 34
    and the Mental Health Act **190**.11
    right to family life **245**.1
    of sexually exploited children **202**.23
    spending power falling **207**.8
    support for pregnant teenagers **182**.16

support to prevent child crime **223**.32
    see also lone parents; parents; stepfamilies
Family Lives report on sexualisation of children **238**.14-15
family planning
    Millennium Development Goals **218**.39
    and population control **218**.26-7
    see also birth control; contraception
family planning clinics, use by teenagers **182**.1-2
family therapy **252**.19; **249**.21
farm produce surplus harvested for charities **242**.39
farming *see* agriculture; organic farming
fashion industry
    and body image **234**.5-6, 11
    and fur trade **233**.19
    and living wage **229**.13
fast food
    and depression **252**.24
    litter **242**.13
fats in diet **205**.1, 3, 24
    food labelling **205**.11
    need to reduce fat content of food **205**.18
    taxes on unhealthy food **241**.20-21
fathers
    and childcare **221**.5
    contact with children after family break-up **191**.11
    parenting roles **191**.30-33
    paternity leave **183**.18, 22, 24; **191**.34-5, 39; **221**.4-5
    post-natal depression **190**.16-17
    teenage fathers **182**.17
    work-family balance **183**.22-3; **191**.34-5
fatty acids
    omega 3 **214**.29, 33
    in red meat **214**.35
Featherstone, Lynn **234**.20-21, 37
Feed-in Tariffs **204**.19, 36
feelings
    after bereavement **192**.1-2, 3, 9-10, 11, 13, 15, 20
    after child abuse **248**.3, 4, 17, 26
fees, university **185**.11, 17, 29, 36
female genital mutilation **224**.3-4, 37
femininity and dieting **234**.8
feminism and sexualisation of girls **238**.39
Ferdinand, Anton **236**.38
Ferdinand, Rio **236**.36, 38
fertility
    effect of abortion **231**.7
    effect of age **247**.2, 4, 5, 6
    effect of cannabis use **186**.16
    problems **247**.1-3, 4
    protecting **247**.2-3, 5
    worldwide **220**.2, 4, 9, 13, 15
fertility drugs **247**.8-9
fertility treatments **247**.3, 7-9
    and multiple births **247**.4
    see also in vitro fertilisation
fetuses
    age of viability **231**.22
    fetal rights **231**.17, 18
    fetal stem cells used to treat stroke victims **211**.33
fighting animals **233**.6, 17, 27

films
    classification **196**.13-16
    influence on young people smoking **188**.25
    public opinion **196**.15-16
filtered cigarettes **188**.10
finance and football **198**.11-12
finance, students *see* students and money matters
financial abuse **224**.1, 3
financial benefits *see* state benefits
financial companies, informing of a death **192**.32
financial education **250**.17, 19, 21
financial implications
    of home ownership **253**.6
    of partner's death **192**.33
financial incentives
    for marriage **191**.2
    for recycling waste **242**.30, 31
financial planning **250**.32-3
    budgeting for debt repayment **250**.37-8
    for old age **239**.14; **250**.36
    see also pensions
financial problems **250**.1, 2, 5, 32-3
    effect on health **250**.29, 33
    for separating couples **244**.33, 38-9
    see also debt
financial skills **250**.1, 2, 18
    young people **250**.17
financial support to adult children by parents
    191.27-8
firearms offences **223**.5
fires caused by smoking **188**.22
first aid treatment for drug abuse effects **199**.14;
    228.2
first-past-the-post electoral system **240**.29
first-time buyers **253**.4
    difficulty raising deposits **253**.1-2
    Help to Buy schemes **253**.7-8,
fish, in diet **205**.3
    labelling rules **205**.12
    vegetarian diet **214**.1
fishing industry
    environmental impact **214**.17, 25-6
    and sustainability **193**.30; **218**.23
        buying sustainable fish **205**.32
fit notes **183**.8
fitness
    and health **241**.1-5, 8
    lack of fitness **241**.7, 13
    obese people **241**.17
    outdoor fitness equipment **241**.36-7
    Zombies, Run! fitness app **241**.38-9
    see also exercise
Fitspo (Fitspiration) **249**.29, 30
five-a-day fruit and vegetable consumption **205**.1,
    2, 17
flags, Union Jack **240**.4-5
flashbacks about child abuse **248**.5
flexible working **183**.16-27
    effect of recession **183**.1
    fathers **183**.22; **191**.34, 39
    and gender equality **221**.24
    mothers **191**.36
    options **183**.17, 18

statistics **183**.20
flexitarian diet **214**.1
flood management **218**.6, 23
flour, labelling rules **205**.11-12
fluid intake **205**.27-8
    during exercise **241**.26
fly ash from waste incineration **242**.36
fly-tipping **242**.8-9, 10, 12
foetus *see* fetuses
foil provision to heroin users **228**.26
food
    in the Army **213**.1
    from cloned animals **211**.10-19
        public attitudes **211**.6
        safety **211**.18, 19
    global food system **218**.29-30
    GM food *see* genetically modified (GM) food
    hunger *see* hunger
    in-vitro meat **211**.20-21
    labelling costs **207**.29
    and mental health **190**.3; **252**.24, 25
    organic **205**.30, 33, 34-6
    supplies
        and climate change **216**.6-7, 10
        and factory farming **233**.8
        and GM crops **208**.19, 23-4, 32, 34-6
        and meat production **214**.5, 16
        and population growth **220**.3-4, 6
    tax on unhealthy food **241**.20-21
    UK regional specialities **240**.3
    see also diet; eating disorders; healthy eating;
meat consumption; vegetarian food
food additives **205**.14-16
    organic food **205**.34
food advertising and children **205**.38
food industry
    and climate change **205**.30
    and the economy **205**.29-30
    need to reduce salt and fat in food **205**.18
    and tackling childhood obesity **241**.20
food intake and overweight **241**.15-16
food labelling
    date labels **242**.14, 15
    ethical labelling costs **207**.29
    GM food **208**.8
    misleading claims **205**.39
    nutritional information **205**.13
    organic food **205**.33
    regulations **205**.11-12
    salt content **205**.26
food and nutrition **205**.1-28
    balanced diet **205**.2-3, 4-5
    see also diet; healthy eating; nutrition;
vegetarianism
food poisoning **205**.5
food poverty in UK **235**.17
food production, environmental impact **205**.30;
    214.16, 17, 18-19, 20-21
food safety **205**.5
    genetically modified food **208**.2, 24
    and organic farming **205**.34, 36
food security
    and GM crops **208**.19,23-4, 34-6

food standards and labelling **205**.11-12
Food Standards Agency (FSA) and GM food **208**.7
food waste **205**.31, 32; **242**.3, 14-16
    anaerobic digestion plant **242**.38
    restaurant doggy box scheme **242**.39
football
    Asian players **198**.24
    and ethnic minorities **236**.12
    finance **198**.11-12
    and homophobia **198**.25, 26
    and racism **236**.9, 12, 13, 15, 25, 38, 39
    and violence **198**.13
    WAGS (wives and girlfriends) **198**.15-17
force feeding of anorexia sufferer **249**.38-9
forced labour **229**.15; **227**.29-3-0
    and human trafficking **229**.17
forced marriages **224**.3, 14-15, 36-7; **244**.3, 12-14
    action against **220**.30
    of children **248**.24-5
    and Islam **215**.12
forced migration **220**.36-7
forced retirement **183**.14-15
Ford factory equal pay strike **221**.35, 36
foreign holidays, attitudes to **222**.2
foreign nationals
    deportation and the Human Rights Act **229**.4-5
    prisoners **223**.25
    using NHS **251**.23, 24
forests
    and climate change **216**.11, 14-15
    dryland forests **218**.21
    empty forest syndrome **193**.20
    protection **193**.4
    rainforest destruction **193**.1, 5
    rainforest protection, UN programme **218**.20-21
    restoration **193**.15
    see also deforestation
40 Days for Life campaign **231**.34, 35
fossil fuels **204**.6, 25
    energy industry statistics **204**.1
    subsidies **204**.4
    see also oil
fostering
    as alternative to abortion **231**.8
    foster parents' refusal to promote homosexual
lifestyle **225**.34
foundation stage education
    and character skills **219**.34-5
    and social mobility **219**.17-18
4G mobile spectrum **230**.1
Foyer Foundation **189**.25
France
    AIDS strategy support **243**.28
    ban on burqa wearing **215**.39
    health care **251**.9
    and sexualisation of children **238**.27-8
Frank anti-drug helpline **186**.26-7
fraud
    costs of **207**.21-2
    and online information **245**.21-2
free schools **209**.19-21
    and faith schools **215**.21-2
free speech **196**.1-12
    and the Internet **230**.37, 38-9

versus political correctness **236**.35-7
free trade **226**.13-14, 29-30, 33
    and employment **226**.13-14
    negative effects **226**.13-14, 32
    and poverty **226**.14, 29-30, 33
    see also trade liberalisation
freedom of expression **196**.37
    global public opinion **229**.11-12
    and the Internet **230**.37, 38-9
    and pornography **246**.3
    versus privacy **229**.5
freedom of information **196**.38
    and the Internet **230**.37, 38-9
freedom of the press, global study **196**.1-2
freedom from surveillance **196**.38
freight transport trends **200**.22
freshwater resources **193**.5
    impact of climate change **216**.6, 10
Friends and Family Test (NHS care) **251**.33
Friends of the Earth
    opposition to non-agricultural market access
      226.15-16
    views on free trade **226**.15
fringe medicine *see* complementary medicine (CM)
fronto-temporal dementia **239**.28
fronto-temporal lobar degeneration (FTLD) **201**.10
fruit and vegetable consumption **205**.1, 2, 17
fruit juices **205**.28
    labelling rules **205**.12
FSA (Food Standards Agency) and GM food **208**.7
FTSE 100 companies, use of tax havens **227**.35-6
fuel cells **204**.27, 38
fuel efficient homes **235**.16
fuel poverty **204**.23; **218**.3; **235**.15-16
    and microgeneration **204**.36
full-time parents, stress **191**.35
fundamentalism, Islamic **212**.32
funding
    AIDS strategy **243**.7, 27, 28-9
    EMA **209**.17, 18
    faith schools **215**.17
    further education **209**.17
    higher education **185**.17, 35-6; **209**.29, 31-2, 35
      see also tuition fees
    homeopathy on the NHS **195**.16, 17-22, 24-5
    NHS **251**.1, 36
      funding crisis **251**.34-5, 38
      public opinions **251**.20-21
    road network **200**.6, 7, 9-10
    of social care **239**.20-23
    sport
      disability sports **198**.18, 20, 21
      funding cuts **198**.6-7
funerals **192**.30-31, 34-7
fungus able to break down plastic **242**.27
fur trade **233**.3-4, 18-19
further education, funding **209**.17
    benefits of **183**.33, 34

G

G8 summit, climate change agreement **216**.37
Galapagos Islands, environmental change **193**.24-5
gambling **203**.1-39
   addiction *see* problem gambling
   definition **203**.5
   effects **203**.21-2, 28-9
   forms of **203**.4
   giving up **203**.6-7
   history of **203**.5
   online gambling **203**.28-9
      participation rates **203**.4
      women **203**.35-6
      young people **203**.17
   participation in **203**.3-4
      young people **203**.12, 16-17
   problem gamblers *see* problem gambling
   reasons for **203**.1, 9, 21, 32-3
   social context **203**.32-3
   women **203**.26, 35-6
   young people **203**.9-18
      Internet gambling **203**.16-18
      problem gambling **203**.12, 15, 16, 20
      reasons for gambling **203**.9
   see also casinos; National Lottery; problem
gambling
GamCare **203**.11
gamete donation *see* egg donation; sperm donation
gamete intra-fallopian transfer (GIFT) **247**.8
gaming
   and bullying **232**.25
   women **230**.2
gaming machines **203**.4
gamma-butyrolactone (GBL) **194**.9
gamma-hydroxybutyrate (GHB) **194**.9
gang injunctions (gangbos) **223**.35-6
gangs **189**.28
   and crime **223**.6-7, 13-15, 35-6
Gap Action Programme, WHO **201**.36
gap years **185**.31; **183**.20
   popular destinations **222**.19
   volunteering **240**.36
Gardasil (HPV vaccine) **237**.26, 27
garment industry, campaign for living wage **229**.13
gas
   green **204**.24
   natural gas industry trends **204**.1
gasification **204**.6
gastric surgery for weight loss *see* bariatric surgery
gay couples *see* same-sex relationships
gay marriage see same-sex marriage
gay men
   and adoption **191**.22-5
   and ageing **239**.10-11
   awareness of gay feelings **225**.1
   and blood donation **225**.36-7
   and HIV **243**.7, 8, 21-2
   testing for STIs and HIV **243**.9
   young people, mental health problems **201**.3
   see also homosexuality
GCSEs

ethnic minorities' performance **236**.10
as predictor of degree results **219**.32
reform **209**.6
GDP (Gross Domestic Product) as poor measure of
living standards **226**.14
gender **221**.1, 11
   and alcohol consumption, young people **194**.2
   and alcohol-related deaths **194**.13
   and attitudes to higher education **209**.27
   and attitudes to school **209**.11
   and colour preferences **221**.7-8
   and compulsive shopping **207**.6
   and education *see* gender and education
   and employment **221**.1-2, 18, 19, 27-9, 37
      see also women in the workforce
   and gambling **203**.16
   and graduate unemployment **185**.32
   and health issues **252**.9-10
   and HIV sufferers in UK **243**.14
   and household tasks **221**.6
   and Internet usage **230**.2-4
   and media usage **210**.12
   and mental health problems **190**.18-19
   and the news **210**.6-8
   and parental roles **191**.30-32
   and pay *see* gender pay gap
   and smoking **188**.1
   and suicide **199**.24, 28, 32
   and work **221**.27-9
   see also gender pay gap; men; women
gender abortions **231**.18, 30-31
gender assignation **225**.8
gender-based violence *see* domestic abuse; rape
gender dysphoria **225**.20, 21-2
gender and education
   attitudes to school **209**.11
   higher education **185**.14; **209**.27
gender equality
   international initiatives **221**.2
   and Islam **215**.12
   legal rights **221**.2, 3
   Olympic Games **198**.19
Gender Equality Duty (GED) **225**.7
gender identity clinics **225**.20
   Tavistock and Portman service **225**.21, 22, 23
gender identity disorder **225**.20
gender inequality **221**.1-2, 33-5, 37
   at work **221**.1-2, 18, 19, 27, 37
   definition **221**.11
   worldwide **221**.1-2, 33-9
gender pay audits **221**.24
gender pay gap **221**.22-5, 27-8, 35-6, 37
Gender Recognition Act 2004 **225**.6, 20, 27
gender quotas, company boards **221**.16, 21
gender stereotyping **221**.11, 33
   children **238**.3, 14, 33-4
   and employment **221**.23, 28, 29
   and sexualisation **238**.3, 14
   and toys **221**.7-8; **238**.33-4
gender variant **225**.20
genderqueer **225**.20
gene doping **198**.30
gene mapping **208**.13

gene splicing *see* genetic modification

gene therapy as cure for HIV **243**.32, 33

general practitioners *see* GPs (general practitioners)

generalised anxiety disorder (GAD) **206**.11, 14-15

genes

    and anxiety **206**.3

    and depression **190**.2, 4, 12-13

        bipolar disorder **190**.11, 12-13

        teenage depression **190**.25

    and divorce **244**.32

    and eating disorders **249**.5

    and gambling addiction **203**.30-31

    human genes implanted into animals **233**.39

    and lifespan **239**.2

    and mental health **201**.33

    and obesity **241**.16

    and sexual orientation **225**.1-2

    and stress **206**.30-31

genetic diseases

    and sex selection **247**.35

    testing of embryos **247**.8

    and three-parent IVF **247**.29-34

genetic modification

    applications **208**.6, 19-22, 37-8

    arguments against **208**.3-4, 5, 17

    arguments for **208**.2, 3, 17

    definition **208**.1, 3

    and the environment **208**.20, 22, 29

    generations of plants **208**.1-2

    human cells transplanted into animals **233**.39

    method **208**.14

    risks **208**.17

    testing **208**.1

    see also genetically modified animals; genetically

modified crops; genetically modified food

genetic resources, international cooperation **193**.12

genetic testing of embryos **247**.8

genetically modified (GM) animals **208**.3, 13-14,

    37-9

    chickens **208**.14, 37-8

    experiments on **208**.37-8

    fish **214**.25-6

    salmon **208**.31, 39

genetically modified (GM) crops **208**.1-2

    and animal feed **208**.8, 24

    arguments for and against **208**.5, 9-10, 17, 34

    crop area **208**.9, 10

    cross-contamination **208**.24, 26

    developing countries **208**.10

    and food supply **208**.19, 23-4, 32, 34-6

    risks **208**.27-8

    UK **208**.5, 17-18

genetically modified (GM) food **208**.5-8

    arguments against **208**.23-4, 31-2

    effects on health **208**.5, 8, 19-20

    public attitudes to **208**.18, 29-30; **211**.6

    safety **208**.1, 2, 7

genital herpes **237**.20

genital warts **237**.20

Genuine Occupational Requirement and sexual

orientation **225**.28

geothermal energy **204**.3, 27

Germany

    AIDS strategy support **243**.28

    health care **251**.9

    privacy rights **245**.4

Getting it Right campaign **197**.39

Ghana

    impact of free trade **226**.29, 32

    income growth **235**.30

    withdrawal of aid due to anti-gay laws **225**.14

ghost tourism **222**.16

Gibson inquiry into use of torture **229**.22, 23

GIFT (gamete intra-fallopian transfer) **247**.8

Gilderdale, Kay **217**.27-8, 29, 34

ginger bullying **232**.16

Girlguiding UK

    body confidence campaign **234**.34

    survey on media pressure on girls **238**.13

girls and young women

    aspiring to be WAGS **198**.15-17

    attitudes to school **209**.11

    and beauty pageants **238**.28-30

    and body image **234**.9, 25-6, 31

    and child labour **202**.5

    child soldiers **202**.32, 35-6

    and cosmetic surgery **234**.33, 34

    and cricket **198**.4

    and education **221**.31-2, 35, 38-9

        effect on population control **220**.7

        programmes in developing countries **229**.27-8

    HPV vaccination **237**.27, 28, 29-31

    media influences **238**.3, 13

    and parental separation **244**.36

    and prostitution **246**.27-8, 34-8

    and sexual violence **238**.17

    sexualisation of **221**.9-10; 8-9, 27-39

    single-sex education **221**.31-2

    toy preferences **221**.7-8

    violence against **224**.28-31

girls' schools **221**.31-2

Girls' Union **246**.21

Give Yourself a Chance campaign **234**.34

glamping **222**.20

glass ceiling **221**.21-2

Gleaning Network UK **242**.39

global financial crisis **235**.13-14

Global Media Monitoring Project **210**.6-8

Global Partnership on Forest Restoration (GPFLR)

    193.15

global poverty **235**.23-39

    statistics **235**.23, 24

global targets on child protection **248**.32-3

global trade **226**.26-39

global warming **216**.8, 9; **218**.19

    measurement **216**.26-7

    see also climate change; energy efficiency;

greenhouse gas

    emissions

globalisation **226**.1-25

    definition **226**.1, 13

    effects of **226**.2, 13, 20-21, 24-5

    and ethical consumerism **207**.23

    need for international cooperation **226**.17-19, 21,

    22-5

    and trade **226**.26-39

GM crops *see* genetically modified (GM) crops
golden rice **208**.19, 29, 35
gonorrhoea **237**.20-21, 24-5
'good' deaths **192**.8, 24
Goodger, Lauren **234**.6-7
Goody, Jade, and cervical cancer screening **237**.32
Google
    censorship requests from governments **196**.29
    data requests from governments **245**.13
    Google Circles **245**.3
    Street View **210**.33; **245**.38-9
    withdrawal from China **196**.27-8, 29, 30
Gosling, Ray **217**.29
gossip magazines and eating disorders **249**.28
gourmand syndrome **249**.8
government, UK **240**.3, 21, 26
    body confidence campaign **234**.20-21, 37, 39
    control of broadcasters **196**.18-19
    devolved government **240**.27-8
    domestic violence definitions **224**.34-7
    ethnic minority members **236**.11
    finance, and smoking **188**.22, 23
    funding for disabled children **197**.36
    government ministers **240**.26
    healthy behaviour promotion **234**.11-12
    and the monarchy **240**.22
    open data policies **245**.12-13
    and religion **215**.6
    women's representation **221**.13, 15, 20, 37
    see also Parliament
government policies
    on alcohol **194**.33
    child poverty strategy **235**.19
    on crime **223**.23-5
        gang crime **223**.13-15
    on drugs **186**.4, 35-6; **228**.24-7
        see also classification of drugs
    on education **209**.17, 18, 19, 24
        academies **209**.25, 26
    and financial pressures **250**.32
    on genetically modified crops **208**.5
    on higher education **185**.25
    on home ownership **253**.7-8, 9, 25
    on homelessness **189**.8, 34
    and homeopathy **195**.23, 24, 25, 26-7
    on house building **253**.24
    and integrated healthcare **195**.23
    on Internet porn regulation **246**.15-16
    on mental health **201**.5
    and obesity **205**.20-21
    on preventing violence against women and girls
        224.28-31
    on prostitution **246**.17-18
    on public health **219**.13
    renewable energy **204**.4, 7-8, 15-16
    sensible drinking guidelines *see* daily benchmarks
on alcohol consumption
    on smoking **188**.33-5
    on social mobility **219**.17-21
    waste management **242**.1-4, 9
    welfare reforms **235**.9, 10
government targets on homelessness **189**.8

governments
    control of the Internet **196**.32-5
    data requests to Google **245**.13
    Internet censorship requests **196**.29
GPs (general practitioners)
    and anxiety sufferers **252**.15
    asking about patient's alcohol consumption
        194.33, 37-8
    diagnosing depression **190**.31
    and eating disorders **249**.21, 33
    and young people **252**.5
    see also doctors
graduates
    destinations **185**.31-2
    earnings **183**.34; **185**.21, 32-4
    employment **185**.31-2, 36-7
        effect of recession **183**.1-2, 35-6
    options after graduating **185**.30-31
    starting salaries **183**.36
graffiti, racist **236**.14
grandparents **191**.14-17
    and childcare **191**.15, 16-17
Grannynet website **239**.38
grants, student **185**.2; **250**.24
Great Ocean Conveyor **216**.8
Great Pacific Garbage Patch **242**.21
green belt land threats **253**.38-9
green cars *see* fuel efficient cars
green gas **204**.24
Green Tobacco Sickness **188**.39
green tourism *see* ecotourism; responsible travel;
sustainable tourism
greenhouse effect **216**.1
greenhouse gases
    emission reduction targets **216**.7, 33
    emission trends **216**.7
    emissions
        from food production **205**.30
        from livestock farming **214**.17, 18, 19, 21
        from transport **200**.14, 15, 22
        from waste incineration **242**.34-5
    and GM crops **208**.22
    see also carbon dioxide emissions
Greenhouse project **253**.37
Greenland ice sheet **216**.15
greenwashing **222**.24
grey squirrels **193**.38
grief **192**.1-2, 3-4
    before death **192**.6
    and depression **239**.32
    public **192**.7-8
    and young people **192**.9-23
Griffin, Nick **236**.37
grocery shopping, online **207**.10
grooming **202**.21, 25; **246**.34, 35-6; **248**.30, 31
    online **230**.23-4
Gross Domestic Product (GDP) as poor measure of
living standards **226**.14
ground source heat pumps **204**.35
growth hormones and sports drug abuse **198**.30
Guantánamo Bay **212**.33-5
    torture of detainees **212**.36-7
guided busways **200**.30, 32

Guiding Principles on Business and Human Rights (UN) **227**.27, 28
guilt
    children's feelings after bereavement **192**.13
    and pornography use **246**.2
    and post traumatic stress disorder **201**.21
gun crime **223**.5
Guttman, Ludwig **198**.20-21
Gypsies and Travellers, discrimination against **236**.21-2
    Scotland **236**.22

H

HAART *see* antiretroviral therapy
habitat loss **193**.1
    see also deforestation
Haiti, debt and disater **226**.6
Halal slaughter **233**.16
halls of residence **209**.30
hallucinogens (psychedelics) **228**.3-4, 14
handbag dogs **233**.4
hangovers **194**.7
happiness
    and health, teenagers **241**.8
    and marriage **244**.10
harassment
    definition **221**.3; **225**.28
    by journalists, Editor's Code **210**.28
    racial **236**.1-2
    on grounds of sexual orientation **225**.28
hardening hypothesis (stopping smoking) **188**.17
hashish (cannabis resins) **186**.2, 7, 9
hate crime
    anti-Muslim **215**.28-30; **236**.14, 24
        see also Islamophobia
    homophobic **225**.29, 30-31, 32
hazardous waste **218**.12
    EU trade **242**.18-19
    illegal dumping **242**.10-11
HDAC inhibitors **243**.34
HDTV **210**.11, 14
headteachers, concern about extremism in schools **212**.12
health **252**.1-39
    and alcohol
        benefits **194**.18
        risks **194**.6, 7, 15, 17, 18, 19, 22-3
    and anxiety **206**.10
    and body image **234**.10, 11
    and cannabis **186**.15-17, 28-9
    and car travel **200**.1, 23
    children's rights **229**.24
    and climate change **216**.7, 10
    and divorce **244**.33
    and drug abuse **228**.12-13
    exercising with health problems **198**.23
    and fuel poverty **235**.15-16
    and GM crops **208**.19-20, 29
    HIV sufferers **243**.18, 30-31
    and homelessness **189**.12-13
    inequalities **235**.6-7
    and marriage **244**.10
        child marriage **244**.15
    and meat consumption **214**.16, 34-5
    and money worries **250**.29, 33
    and obesity **241**.15, 17
    older people **239**.3-4, 8, 27
        depression **239**.31-2
        health problems **239**.4, 24-6
        lesbian, gay and bisexual people **239**.10
        see also dementia
    and organic produce **205**.34, 36
    and physical activity **241**.1-5, 9, 32, 33-4
    and population growth **220**.2
    in pregnancy **182**.15
        employment rights **191**.37
    and salt intake **205**.25-6
    and smoking **188**.5-12, 15, 18, 19, 22
        benefits of giving up **188**.6, 9
        passive smoking **188**.5, 10-11, 12
        in pregnancy **188**.11, 31
    and social class **219**.11-13
    teenage parents and their children **182**.27
    tobacco pickers **188**.39
    travel health advice **222**.10
    and vegetarian diets **205**.37; **214**.4-5, 9, 12, 28-33, 36-9
    and waste incinerators **242**.36
    see also mental health; mental illness; sexual health
health care **251**.1-39
    clinics in schools, Youth Parliament manifesto **240**.38
    discrimination, disabled people **197**.30, 38-9
    NHS *see* NHS
    sources of advice for young people **252**.4-5
    see also care services for older people
Health Check programme **251**.3
Health and Safety at Work Act and stress **206**.25, 28
health service *see* National Health Service
Health and Social Care Act **251**.3-4, 25-6, 29
health tourists **251**.23
health warnings on cigarette packs **188**.29
Health and Well-being Boards **251**.26, 31
Healthwatch **251**.26, 31-2
healthy eating **205**.2-3, 4-5, 17-18, 23
    advice linked to eating disorders **249**.21
    and ageing **239**.27
    and the environment **205**.31
    and meat consumption **214**.34-5
    and mental health **252**.25
    and schools **205**.6-7; **252**.30
    and stress **206**.33
    and vegetarian diets **205**.37-8; **214**.28-30, 33, 36, 37, 38-9
    see also diet; food and nutrition
Healthy magazine, airbrushing **234**.27-8
Healthy Lives, Healthy People White Paper **219**.13
healthy weight maintenance *see* weight management
hearing loss, older people **239**.25
heart
    effects of alcohol **194**.18

effects of salt intake **205**.25
effects of smoking **188**.7
heart attack risk of men having affairs **244**.33
heart disease **239**.25
    and animal research **233**.35-6
    protective effect of alcohol **194**.18
    and red meat consumption **214**.35
    and smoking **188**.7
    and stress **206**.4
    and vegetarian diet **214**.31-2
heart transplant, Britain's first **251**.2
heat pumps, microgeneration **204**.35
Heavily Indebted Poor Countries (HIPC) initiative **226**.5-6
heavy drinking *see* alcohol abuse
hens
    battery farmed **233**.3, 7
    genetically modified **208**.14, 37-8
hepatitis B **237**.21
herbal cannabis (marijuana/grass) **186**.2, 9
    see also skunk
herbal medicine **195**.3-4, 9, 10-13
    benefits **195**.11
    buying over the Internet **195**.8, 39
    definition **195**.11
    effectiveness of **195**.33
    history of **195**.10
    and the NHS **195**.11
    how it works **195**.11
    public attitudes to **195**.34-5
    phobia treatment **206**.13
    registration scheme **195**.4, 35, 38
    regulation **195**.4, 33, 34-5, 36, 37-8
    reporting adverse reactions **195**.38-9
    safety **195**.2, 12-13, 37-9
heredity *see* genes
heroin, signs of use **228**.14-15
herpes, genital **237**.20
hetero-normative attitudes **225**.11, 27
hidden child abuse **248**.8
hidden disabilities **197**.8-9
hidden homelessness **189**.4, 23
high blood pressure (hypertension) **241**.4
    and salt intake **205**.25
high earners, attitudes to pay **227**.24-5
high-intensity training **241**.27-8
high-speed rail **200**.35, 36, 37-9
higher education **209**.27-39
    alternatives options **185**.16-17
    black students, employment prospects **236**.19-20
    and business **185**.34-6
    degree results and school background **209**.12
    and earning power **185**.1, 21-2; **183**.34
    and ethnic minorities **236**.10
    funding **185**.17, 35-6; **209**.2, 31-2, 35; **250**.22-5
    and gender **185**.14
    government policy **185**.25
    parental encouragement **209**.36
    reasons for not participating **209**.27, 28
    record number of applications **209**.37-8
    reform **185**.20-21
    and social class **209**.34-5
    student life **209**.30-33

value of **185**.1, 15-17
    young people's attitudes to **209**.27-8
    see also further education; graduates; students; universities
highly active antiretroviral therapy *see* antiretroviral therapy
Hinduism **215**.2
    and abortion **231**.19
    and faith schools **215**.21
    funerals **192**.35
    and pornography **246**.1
    and vegetarianism **214**.6
historic child abuse **248**.36
HIV (Human Immunodeficiency Virus) **237**.21; **243**.1-39
    cure **243**.32-5, 37-9
    definition **243**.1
    and discrimination **243**.15-17
    disability classification **197**.1
    education **243**.10-11
    effects **243**.2
    infection rate
        UK **243**.5
        worldwide **243**.6, 26-7
    living with HIV **243**.14-25
        children **243**.23-5
        older people 19-20, 30-31
    prevalence **243**.2
    and quality of life **243**.18-19
    risk groups **243**.6-7, 8-9
    symptoms **243**.2
    testing for **243**.3, 9, 35, 36
    timeline **243**.7
    transmission **243**.1-2
        criminalisation **243**.11
        mother-to-child **243**.1-2, 25
    treatments **243**.3-4
        worldwide access **243**.6
    UK statistics **243**.2, 5, 14-15
    worldwide statistics **243**.6-7
    and young people **243**.23-5
    see also AIDS
HOLD (Home Ownership for People with Long-Term Disabilities) **253**.8
holidays
    Army leave **213**.2
    attitudes to **222**.2
    costs **222**.5, 6-7
    destinations
        Britain as holiday destination **222**.2-3, 5, 11
        gap year travel **222**.19
        reasons for choice **222**.2-3, 11
        trends **222**.1
    see also responsible tourism; tourism
Holyoake, George **215**.15
home building **253**.16
    affordable homes **253**.28
    council targets reduced **253**.27
    funded by councils selling high-value properties **253**.29-30
    on green belt **253**.38-9
    terraced houses **253**.31
home care services and older people's human

rights **229**.33-4
home environments and educational attainment
   219.27, 33
home ownership
   difficulties for young people **253**.2-3, 5
   Help to Buy schemes **253**.6, 7-8, 9
   pros and cons **253**.6
   trends **253**.3
Home Ownership for People with Long-Term
Disabilities (HOLD) **253**.8
home testing for HIV **243**.36
homelessness **189**.1-39
   asylum seekers **189**.14-15
   causes **189**.5, 6, 24, 26, 27
   and children **189**.29-32
   definitions **189**.1, 3
   and drug use **189**.10-11, 13, 35-6
   effects **189**.5
   and employment **189**.33
   ex-service personnel **189**.6; **213**.35
   and health **189**.12-13
   government policies **189**.8, 34
   help for homeless people **189**.34-9
   hidden homeless **189**.4, 23
   legislation **189**.1-2, 34
   and local authorities **189**.1-2, 34
   and mental health **189**.9-11
   priority needs groups **189**.2, 3
   rough sleeping **189**.4, 16-17
     government targets **189**.8
     and mental health **189**.11
     young people **189**.23
   statistics **189**.3-4, 16-17, 21, 23; **253**.23
   trends **189**.8
   young people **189**.21-32
     housing rights **189**.24-5
     reasons for leaving home **189**.24, 26, 27
   see also street homelessness;   temporary
accommodation
homeopathy
   arguments against **195**.25, 27
   arguments for **195**.22, 32
   dangers of **195**.30-31
   definition **195**.24
   and the NHS **195**.16-22, 24-5
homestays (holidays) **222**.24
homicide crimes **223**.4-5
homophobia
   in football **198**.25, 26
   homophobic bullying **225**.9, 29; **232**.12-13
     and schools **225**.7, 8
   prevention strategies **232**.15
homophobic crime **225**.29, 30-31, 32
homosexuality **225**.1-4
   causes **225**.1-2, 15-16
   'curing' **225**.2, 16, 17-18
   and human rights **229**.31-2
   self-awareness of **225**.1
   see also gay men; lesbians; LGBT people; same-
sex relationships
honey, labelling rules **205**.12
honour based violence **224**.3
horizontal occupational segregation **221**.27

hormone disrupting chemicals, effect on wildlife
193.16-17
hormones
   abuse in sport **198**.29-30
   and ageing **239**.1
   and depression **190**.2
horses
   fighting **233**.27
   Przewalski's horse conservation **233**.26
Hospital Plan (1962) **251**.2
hospitals
   A&E waiting times **251**.17
   admissions under Mental Health Act **201**.38
   Britons hospitalised overseas **222**.15
   care standards **251**.8
     elderly patients **251**.11-13
     Friends and Family test **251**.33
   post mortems **192**.31
   treatment for self-harm **199**.13-14, 15
hostels for homeless people **189**.17, 31-2, 35
hotel industry
   eco-lodges **222**.24
   and ethics **222**.31-2
hours of work
   long working hours and stress on parents **206**.22-
3
   young workers **183**.28-9
   see also employment
House of Lords, and bishops **215**.6
household debt **250**.5, 11
household waste **218**.11, 12; **242**.22
   food waste **242**.14-16
   government policies **242**.3-4
   incineration **242**.34-6
   recycling **242**.23-4, 30, 31
   see also composting waste; waste management
households
   gender roles **221**.6
   low-income **235**.5-8
   minimum standard income **235**.5
   spending **207**.7
   spending power falling **207**.8
   see also families; homeless households
housework
   and gender **221**.6
   housework sharing and risk of divorce **244**.32
housing **253**.1-39
   building *see* home building
   and climate change **216**.29-30
   disability rights **197**.21-2
   disabled children **197**.37
   empty homes **253**.18, 32-5
   energy efficient **235**.16
   home design and privacy **245**.2
   immigrants and social housing **220**.28, 29
   policies **253**.18, 24, 25-6
   and poverty **235**.7
   priority needs households **189**.2, 3
   problems for separating couples **244**.38-9
   problems for young people **191**.26, 27
     mental health sufferers **201**.29
   rented sector **253**.1, 10-13
   shortage **253**.16, 19-20, 23

social housing *see* social housing
students **185**.7
sustainable **253**.36, 37
young people **189**.24-5
see also affordable housing; home ownership; homelessness; rural housing; temporary accommodation
How Good is Porn campaign **246**.6
How to Look Good Naked (TV programme) **234**.19
HPV (human papilloma virus) **237**.20, 26
and cancer **237**.26
vaccination programme **251**.3
vaccines **237**.26-7, 28, 29-31
human cloning **211**.22-39
arguments for and against **211**.26-7
ethical issues **211**.8-9, 26-7
legislation **211**.25
therapeutic cloning **211**.9, 22-3
human embryos *see* embryos
Human Fertilisation and Embryology Bill **211**.25; **231**.2
human growth hormones (HGHs) and sport **198**.30
human immunodeficiency virus *see* HIV
human reproductive cloning **211**.22, 24-7
Human Reproductive Cloning Act **211**.25
human rights **229**.1-23
and business **227**.27-8
children *see* children's rights
definition **229**.1
and Internet access **230**.38-9
public attitudes to **229**.11-12
water and sanitation **218**.32
Human Rights Act **229**.1-8
arguments against **229**.7-8
arguments for **229**.8
coverage **229**.1-2
and freedom of expression **196**.14
fundamental rights and freedoms **229**.2
and home care **229**.34
myths **229**.3-6
rights to private and family life **245**.1
and sexual orientation **225**.7
Human Rights Risk Atlas **229**.9
human trafficking *see* trafficking
humanism **215**.4
and euthanasia **217**.6
funerals **192**.37
Hungarian immigrants **236**.32
hunger
food poverty, UK **235**.17
impact of biofuels **204**.33-4
Millennium Development Goals **235**.26-7
worldwide **220**.6
hunting
for bushmeat **193**.23
captive animals **193**.17
endangered species **193**.1-2
hybridization **211**.2
see also cross-contamination
hydration **205**.27-8
hydro power **204**.19, 27
hydrogen power **204**.26-7, 38
hyperactivity and food additives **205**.14-15

hypermasculinity **238**.17
hypertension *see* high blood pressure
hypnosis **195**.4
hypnotherapy **252**.15
hypomania **190**.9
hypoxia threat to ocean life **218**.24-5

I

IBRD (International Bank for Reconstruction and Development) **226**.10
ice sheets, impact of climate change **216**.12, 15
ICSI (intra-cytoplasmic sperm injection) **247**.7
ICSID (International Centre for Settlement of Investment Disputes) **226**.10
ICT
education **230**.13
see also computers; Internet
IDA (International Development Association) **226**.9
identity
British *see* British identity
national, impact of globalisation **226**.12
identity fraud **207**.19-20; **230**.24
young people's risk of **245**.21-2
IFC (International Finance Corporation) **226**.10
illegal abortion **231**.12
illegal dumping *see* fly-tipping
ILO *see* International Labour Organisation
images, effects on young people's smoking **188**.24-6
IMF *see* International Monetary Fund
imitation as indirect racism **236**.28
immigration
attitudes to **220**.22-3, 26, 27-8
David Cameron's speech **220**.30-31
and domestic violence victims **224**.37
European Union **220**.31
immigrants' use of NHS **251**.23, 24
integration of immigrants **240**.15-16, 19
and population diversity **240**.15
and social housing **220**.28, 29
UK **220**.21-2, 24-5
see also asylum seekers; ethnic minorities; migrant workers; migration
immune system
and complementary therapies **195**.7
and fertility **247**.8
implants, contraceptive **237**.7
import tariffs **226**.26-7
importation of indecent articles **196**.23
imprisonment *see* prison
in-law relationships and risk of divorce **244**.32
in vitro fertilization (IVF) **247**.7, 9-10
experience of **247**.11-12
numbers of babies born **247**.13
and older women **247**.22-6
and same-sex couples **247**.27
sex offender's right to IVF **247**.28
three-parent IVF to prevent genetic diseases **247**.29-34
using unused embryos for research **211**.31

in vitro maturation **247**.8
in vitro meat **211**.20-21
inactivity **241**.1, 7, 16
    children **241**.35
    health risks **241**.1-2
incentives for recycling **242**.31
incineration of waste **242**.34-6
    plant threatening waste pickers' jobs, India
        242.29
    to produce energy **242**.32-3
    Sweden importing waste for energy plants **242**.37
inclusion
    disabled children **197**.36-7
        education **197**.15, 27, 37
    and sport **198**.18-26
    in the workforce **183**.26-7
Income Tax **250**.13
incomes
    and children's educational attainment **219**.22, 23,
        25-6, 27-8, 29-30, 34
    effect on children's character **191**.6
    high earners' attitudes to pay **227**.24-5
    income calculation for debt repayment **250**.37
    inequalities **219**.8, 16; **227**.15, 16
        and Internet access **230**.4, 5
        see also rich-poor gap
    low-income households **235**.5-8
    middle classes **219**.2, 3, 9-10
    minimum standard **235**.3, 5
    minimum wage. young people **183**.28
    perceptions of wage levels **219**.15
    see also earnings; gender pay gap; salaries;
wages
indecency offences **196**.22-3
indecent images **248**.10-11
independence, Scotland **240**.5, 6, 32
independent schools
    and university applications **185**.19
independent shops **207**.28
    threat from supermarkets **207**.26, 27
indeterminate sentences **223**.20
India
    censorship of sexual content on the Internet
        196.37
    child labour **202**.11
    as gap year destination **222**.19
    gender inequality **221**.1
    impact of free trade **226**.30
    plastic bags used in road surfacing **242**.28
    privacy rights **245**.4
    surrogate mothers and health risks **247**.20-21
    waste pickers threatened by incinerator plant
        242.29
indigenous people
    Amazon town ban on tourists **222**.32
    impact of tourism **222**.21-3, 29-30, 33-4
indirect discrimination
    against Gypsies and Travellers **236**.22
    racial **236**.2
    and sexual orientation **225**.28
indirect racism **236**.28
Indonesia, palm oil industry and biodiversity **193**.8-9
induced pluripotent stem cells (iPS cells) **211**.35-7

industry
    costs of smoking **188**.22-3
inequality
    in employment **183**.13
    and the environment **218**.3-4
    gender see gender inequality
    of global resource usage **193**.4
    health **219**.11-13
    of incomes **219**.8, 16
    schools admissions **219**.24
    and social mobility **219**.16
    UK **235**.12, 13
    see also child poverty; poverty; rich-poor gap
Infant Life Preservation Act 1929 **231**.1
infection-triggered auto immune anorexia nervosa
    249.7-8
infertility **247**.1-3, 4
    see also fertility; fertility treatments
information
    evaluating online information **230**.10-12
    online searching and gender **230**.3
    personal, control of **230**.24, 30; **245**.11-27
    security of information and social networking
        210.30-31
    see also Freedom of Information Act
information technology (IT) see computers; Internet
Inglis, Frances **217**.27, 29
inherited wealth **219**.8
injections, contraceptive **237**.7
injured service personnel **213**.2, 7, 8-9, 10-11
innovations of the decade **210**.17-18
insects
    declining numbers **193**.26
        bees and pollinators **193**.27-8
    effect of GM crops **208**.27
    role in ecosystems **193**.26
    stag beetles, London **193**.35
instant messaging (IM)
    and bullying **232**.25
    reporting misuse **232**.36
    support for anxiety sufferers **252**.14-15
institutions, leaving
    as cause of homelessness **189**.6
    and help with housing **189**.25
insulin
    and biotechnology **211**.3
    and sports drug abuse **198**.30, 35
insurance industry and climate change studies
216.18-19
integrated healthcare **195**.23
integration
    British Muslims **240**.17-18
    immigrants **236**.17; **240**.15-16, 19
    into society **215**.9
    racial see racial integration
intellectual impairment **197**.6
intellectual property rights see patents
intensive farming **233**.3, 7-8
interfaith relations, public attitudes to **212**.30-31
Intergovernmental Panel on Climate Change (IPCC)
216.3, 5, 37
    criticism of reports **216**.22-3
internal climate variability **216**.1

internalised stigma about HIV **243**.17
International Bank for Reconstruction and Development (IBRD) **226**.10
International Centre for Settlement of Investment Disputes (ICSID) **226**.10
international companies *see* multinational corporations
International Day of the Girl **248**.24
International Development Association (IDA) **226**.9
International Finance Corporation (IFC) **226**.10
International Labour Organisation (ILO) **229**.14
    and child labour **202**.2, 7-8
    definition of child labour **202**.3
    Global Action Plan **202**.7
    international labour standards **229**.14-16
    report on child labour **202**.15
International Monetary Fund (IMF) **226**.11-12
    and aid **235**.32
International Programme on the Elimination of Child Labour (IPEC) **202**.7
international trade **226**.26-39
    and poverty **226**.28, 29-30, 33
    UK initiatives **226**.28
    see also free trade; globalisation
international unity, need for **226**.18-19
International Women's Day **221**.36
Internet
    access by children **238**.3
    access devices **210**.11, 13
    addiction **230**.14, 16-17, 18
    advertising **230**.5
    broadband access **230**.6-8
    bullying *see* cyberbullying
    and censorship **196**.27-39
        Australia **196**.30
        China **196**.27-8, 30
        government censorship requests **196**.29
        Iran **196**.32, 33
        outsourcing **196**.33-4
        sexual content **196**.36-8
        UK **196**.31
    and child pornography **202**.18
    and child sex abuse **196**.39; **248**.29
    and consumer power **207**.4
    cookies **245**.9-10
    gambling *see* online gambling
    as a human right **230**.38-9
    influence on young people smoking **188**.26
    and innovations of the decade **210**.17
    memorial websites **192**.38-9
    network filters **238**.16, 25, 26; **246**.7, 15-16
    news, and women **210**.8
    and newspapers **210**.19
    online activity **230**.1-5
        children **230**.4-5; **238**.3; **245**.25-7
        and gender **230**.2-4
        older people **230**.5
        young people **230**.4-5, 8-9, 33
    online bullying *see* cyberbullying
    online safety **248**.10-11
    parental controls **238**.5, 25; **245**.26-7
    pornography **246**.3
        children viewing **196**.38; **238**.3-4, 16, 19;

        246.10-11
        filters to block pornography **238**.16, 25, 26; **246**.7, 15-16
        and the law **246**.7-8
        petition against **238**.26
    and privacy **245**.3, 16-27
    pro-eating disorder websites **249**.29-31
    removing online content **232**.35, 36
    safety *see* safety and the Internet
    and self-harm **199**.19
    sexting **238**.23-4
    shopping
        consumer rights **207**.13
        and gender **230**.2, 3-4
        grocery shopping **207**.10
        herbal medicines **195**.8, 39
        international comparisons **210**.15
        safety **207**.10
    support for suicidal people **199**.33, 35
    and travel booking **222**.3
    trends **210**.5
    trolling **232**.32, 37
    usage trends **230**.1-5
    see also child pornography; e-mail; safety and the Internet; social networking
        websites
    see also under online
Internet Service Providers (ISPs) code of practice **246**.15
Internet Service Providers Association (ISPA) criticism of Communications Data Bill **245**.6
Internet Watch Foundation (IWF) **196**.31, 37; **246**.8
    sexual abuse survey **248**.29
internships **219**.20, 37-8
interpersonal therapy **252**.19
intersex **225**.20
intestacy rules **192**.25-6
intra-cytoplasmic sperm injection (ICSI) **247**.7
Inuit and seal hunting **233**.22
invertebrates, conservation needs **193**.26
investment and human rights concerns **229**.9-10
involuntary euthanasia **217**.5
    Belgium **217**.32
involuntary smoking *see* passive smoking
iPads and accessing newspaper content **210**.19
IPCC *see* Intergovernmental Panel on Climate Change
iPS cells (induced pluripotent stem cells) **211**.35-7
IQ **197**.6
    and likelihood of drug abuse **228**.11
Iran
    death penalty **229**.37
    demonstrations via the Internet **196**.32
    government control of the Internet **196**.33
Ireland
    HIV incidence **243**.35
    mandatory reporting of chid abuse **248**.37
    plastic bag charge **242**.25
    see also Northern Ireland
iron in the diet
    red meat **214**.34
    and vegetarian diet **214**.29, 30, 33
Islam **215**.2-3; 9-12

and abortion **231**.19
funerals **192**.34-5
and gender equality **215**.12
and marriage **215**.12
and pornography **246**.1
public perceptions of **212**.4, 30-31
Sharia law **215**.11-12
and terrorism **212**.8-10, 32; **215**.10-11
see also Muslims
Islamophobia **215**.30. 31-2
and the media **215**.33; **236**.23-4
in schools **236**.15
island nations, impacts of climate change **216**.16-17; **220**.38
isolation
as abuse **224**.1
mental health sufferers **201**.6
see also loneliness
ISPA (Internet Service Providers Association)
criticism of Communications Data Bill **245**.6
Italy, AIDS strategy support **243**.29
IVF *see* in vitro fertilization
IVM (in vitro maturation) **247**.8
ivory trade **193**.2, 19
IWF (Internet Watch Foundation) **196**.31, 37

J

jail *see* prison
James, Daniel (assisted suicide case) **217**.21
jams, labelling rules **205**.12
Japan, AIDS strategy support **243**.28
Japanese knotweed **193**.38
Jehovah's Witnesses and abortion **231**.19
Jersey, abortion law **231**.3
Jews (Judaism) **215**.3
and abortion **231**.19
anti-semitism **215**.36
and faith schools **215**.21-2
funerals **192**.34-5
religious slaughter **233**.16
and vegetarianism **214**.6
jihad **212**.32; **215**.11
job adverts and age discrimination **239**.12
Jobcentre Plus, Disability Symbol **197**.26-7
jobs
job satisfaction **183**.3-6
and population growth **220**.6
see also employment; labour market
Joffe, Lord Joel, assisted dying campaign **217**.2
Johns, Owen and Eunice **215**.25, 26; **225**.34
jokes and banter as indirect racism **236**.28
journalists
female **210**.7
regulation **210**.27-8
judicial system
ethnic minorities in legal profession **236**.11-12
treatment of ethnic minorities **236**.9-10
see also criminal justice system
junk food

advertising **205**.38; **241**.20, 21
in children's lunchboxes **205**.10
just-in-time Internet blocking **196**.34
justice system *see* criminal justice system
juvenile arthritis **197**.16-17
juvenile offenders and the death penalty **229**.38

keeping fit *see* fitness
Kenya, population growth **220**.2
Keogh Mortality Review (NHS) **251**.4
Kervorkian, Dr Jack (Dr Death) **217**.2
ketamine **194**.9-10; **228**.5
'legal high' alternative **228**.6
possession, sentencing guidelines **228**.29-30
keyhole surgery **251**.2
Khady, Kolta **248**.25
kidney problems, effect of salt intake **205**.26
knife crime **223**.5, 25, 34
discussion in schools **223**.16-17
mandatory custodial sentences **223**.21, 25
preventing **223**.34
Scotland **223**.6-7
Knowledge Transfer Partnerships **185**.30-31
Knut the polar bear **233**.25
Kooth **252**.15
Kosher meat **233**.16
Korsakoff's syndrome **201**.10
Krishna Avanti Hindu school **215**.21
Kyoto Protocol **216**.34, 37
and transport emissions **200**.15

L

labelling
GM food **208**.8
nanomaterials **208**.16
see also food labelling
labour market, UK **183**.16-17
decline of mid-range jobs **219**.39
fairness in jobs market **219**.18-19, 20
labour migration *see* migrant workers
lacto-ovo-vegetarians **214**.2
lacto-vegetarians **214**.2
lads' magazines and pornography **238**.18
Lake of Stars **240**.35
Laming Review **248**.1
land grabs and human rights **229**.10
landfill **242**.5
policy targets **242**.3
waste of valuable materials **242**.7
landlords
duties to disabled people **197**.22
regulation **253**.11, 12-13
language
and disability
offensive language **197**.28-9
preferred terminology **197**.27

lap dancing clubs **246**.23
Latin America, child soldiers **202**.33
law
    and abortion **231**.1-2, 3, 32
        and disability **231**.20
    and alcohol
        drink-driving **194**.31, 32
        24-hour drinking **194**.20, 21
    animal cloning **211**.11
    animal welfare **233**.1-2, 5-6
    anti-terrorism **212**.19, 20
    and assisted suicide **199**.37-8; **217**.24-38
        arguments against **217**.27
        arguments for **217**.29
        in other countries **217**.2
        in UK **217**.24-6
    and begging **189**.20
    and cannabis **186**.1-2, 4-5, 8, 9, 30-39
    and child protection **248**.1, 34, 35-6
    and cyberbullying **232**.34-5, 37
    and domestic violence **224**.28-9
    and drug driving **228**.26
    and drugs **228**.13, 21-39
        sentencing guidelines **228**.28-31
        see also classification of drugs
    and environmental justice **218**.3, 4
    and euthanasia **217**.24-39
    and film classification **196**.14
    on food additives **205**.15
    food from cloned animals **211**.12
    on food labelling **205**.11-12
    and forced marriages **224**.14-15
    and HIV transmission **243**.11
    and homelessness **189**.1-2, 34
    human cloning **211**.25
    human rights *see* Human Rights Act
    and LGBT people **224**.13; **225**.6-7, 28-39
    libel law reform **210**.37
    and marriage **244**.1-3, 5, 8-9
    and privacy **245**.1-10
    and prostitution **246**.17-19, 21-3
    and religious belief **215**.26-7; **225**.34, 35
    and sexual consent **237**.12-14
    and smoking, children **252**.38-9
    and suicide **199**.27
    and surrogacy **247**.19
    and work-related stress **206**.25, 28-9
    see also legislation
laxative use in eating disorders **249**.2
learning
    effects of cannabis **186**.9-10
    learning styles **209**.1-3
learning disabilities **197**.6-7, 39
    causes **197**.7
    definitions **197**.6-7, 39
    and education **197**.14-15
    and healthcare **197**.38-9
    and forced marriage **244**.12
    statistics **197**.7
    see also disabled people
leather and vegetarianism **214**.13
leave, Army **213**.2
Leeds, Greenhouse project **253**.37

Legal Aid, Sentencing and Punishment of Offenders Bill **223**.25
legal high drugs **228**.1, 36-8
    classification **228**.21
    deaths **252**.32
    and legislation **228**.26-7
    methoxetamine **228**.6
legal profession and ethnic minorities **236**.11-12
legal rights
    and gender equality **221**.2, 3, 35, 36
    young workers **183**.28-9
legalising brothels **246**.26
legalising drugs, arguments for **228**.34
legalising prostitution, effects on trafficking **246**.29
legislation
    Civil Partnership Act **244**.18
    Communications Data Bill **245**.5-8
    Data Protection Act **245**.11
    Equal Pay Act **221**.35-6
    Equality Act **183**.13; **221**.3, 36; **225**.6
    Gender Recognition Act **225**.6, 20, 27
    Marriage (Same-sex Couples) Bill **244**.19-20
    Race Relations Act **236**.1-3, 16, 21
leisure activities
    and mental health **252**.25-6
    Middle Britain **219**.2
Lennox (dog) **233**.12-13
lesbian, gay, bisexual and transgender *see* LGBT people
lesbians
    and ageing **239**.10-11
    and domestic violence **224**.5, 12-13
    human rights **229**.31-2
    young people, mental health problems **201**.3
    see also homosexuality; same-sex relationships
Let Girls Be Girls campaign **238**.8-9
Letting Children be Children (Bailey Review) **238**.2, 5-7, 8, 33, 34
Lewy bodies (dementia) **201**.10
LGBT people **225**.1-39
    attitudes to **225**.11-13
    equality policies, EU **225**.12-13
    and forced marriage **244**.12
    and the law **225**.28-39
    opinions on same-sex marriage **244**.28
    and schools **225**.5-8
    and social exclusion **225**.9
    transgender issues **225**.19-27
    see also gay men; lesbians; same-sex relationships; sexual orientation
libel
    libel actions, celebrities **210**.38
    libel laws reform **210**.37
liberalization of trade   *see* free trade
licence periods (prison sentences) **223**.19-20, 21
licensing hours
    24-hour licensing **194**.20
    and crime **194**.21
LIFE, arguments against HPV vaccination **237**.29-31
life expectancy **239**.1, 3
    and genes **239**.2
    and obesity **241**.15
    and population growth prediction **220**.9

and poverty **219**.13
and smoking **188**.18
and social class **188**.18
life sentences **223**.20, 21
lifestyle
and depression **190**.3
and health **219**.12
middle classes **219**.1-2, 9-10
and stress **206**.18, 32-4
students **209**.30-33
lifetime social tenancies **253**.15
light rail **200**.30, 33-4
light therapy for Seasonal Affective Disorder **190**.6-7
lignocellulose **204**.32
literacy, women, worldwide **221**.37
litter **242**.13, 17
'live for today' attitude **250**.4
liver damage and alcohol **194**.6
Liverpool Care Pathway **251**.15
Livewell menu **214**.22-3
living funerals **192**.36
living together see cohabitation
living wage for garment industry workers **229**.13
living wills see advance directives (living wills)
loans **235**.11-12
to entrepreneurs in developing countries **235**.33
payday loans **250**.5, 6
student **185**.2; **250**.22-5
see also credit; debt
local authorities
approved premises for marriages **244**.2
duty to house **189**.1-2, 34
and ending violence against women and girls **224**.29
home building target reduction **253**.27
open data policy, Manchester **245**.12
responsibilities for under 16s **224**.37
selling properties to fund new home building **253**.29-30
social housing **253**.13-15
Local Authority Social Services Act 1970 **248**.35
local communities, effects of tourism **222**.21-3, 29-30, 33-4
Local Safeguarding Children's Boards **224**.37
logbook loans **235**.12
logging, effect on wildlife **193**.4
loitering and soliciting **246**.21
London
bombings **212**.4, 5
congestion charge **200**.17-18
hostels for homeless people **189**.35
Olympics
and sex trafficking **229**.20
and tourism **222**.12-13
public transport **200**.30
rare wildlife species **193**.35
rough sleepers **189**.16
underground travel, disabled people **197**.12
lone parents
children of **191**.12
and the recession **191**.13
statistics **191**.1, 12
working mothers **191**.36

see also teenage pregnancies
loneliness
and money worries **250**.33
older people **239**.8, 35, 36-7
living with HIV/AIDS **243**.19-20
and stress **206**.18
long-term medical conditions **252**.2, 3, 7-8
see also asthma; cancer; diabetes
Los Angeles, porn film regulations **246**.5
losing weight see weight loss
lotteries **203**.4
see also National Lottery
love and marriage **244**.4
Lovelock, James **220**.12
low income countries **235**.28-30
low income households **235**.5-8
see also child poverty
low income threshold **235**.5
low pay **235**.6
low-tar cigarettes **188**.7, 10
low volume high-intensity training **241**.27-8
loyalty cards and personal data **245**.18-19
lung cancer
and cannabis use **186**.15, 16
and smoking, **188**.6, 8
lung damage
through cannabis use **186**.28
through smoking **188**.5
Luxembourg, assisted dying legislation **217**.2
lynx, reintroduction into Britain **193**.33, 34
Lynx deodorant, advertisements **234**.22

M

M4 bus lane **200**.36
macrobiotic diets **195**.4-5
magazines
airbrushing in *Healthy* magazine **234**.27-8
display of sexualized images **238**.5
diversity award **234**.38
and eating disorders **249**.27, 28
influence on young people smoking **188**.25-6
UK magazine sector **210**.2-3
Vogue and body image **234**.5-6
see also lads' magazines
magnetic resonance imaging (MRI) as alternative to animal research **233**.32
maintained faith schools **209**.22-3
maintenance grants and loans, students **250**.23-4
major (clinical) depression **190**.2, 21
Malawi, withdrawal of aid due to anti-gay laws **225**.14
Maldives
impact of sea level rise **220**.38
impact of tourism **222**.23
male-bonding ceremonies **244**.5
Mali, child labour **202**.10
malnutrition see hunger
Malthus, Thomas **220**.3, 11, 14
Management of Health and Safety at Work Regulations, and stress **206**.25, 28

Management Standards, work-related stress **206**.25-6

management
  gender gap **221**.19-20
  glass ceiling **221**.21-2
Manchester city council, open data policy **245**.12
Mandate Now coalition **248**.38
Mandate to the NHS Commissioners Board **251**.27-8
mandatory life sentences **223**.21
mandatory reporting of child abuse **248**.37, 38
mania **190**.8, 21
manic depression *see* bipolar affective disorder
Many Strong Voices (MSV) project **216**.16
MAOIs (monoamine oxidase inhibitors) **190**.11, 33
Maplecroft Human Rights Risk Atlas **229**.9
mapping genes **208**.13
margin of appreciation, European Court of Human Rights **229**.6
marijuana *see* herbal cannabis
Marine and Coastal Access Act **218**.22
marine environments
  acidification **193**.30
  impacts of tourism **222**.25
  and plastic waste **242**.21, 26-7
  protection **218**.22-3
  threats to **218**.24-5
Marine Strategy Framework Directive **218**.22
marital status and smoking **188**.1
marketing
  and gender stereotyping **238**.34
  parental concerns **238**.35
  and sexualisation of children **238**.6-7, 35
marmalade, labelling rules **205**.12
marriage **244**.1-16
  benefits **244**.10
  ceremonies **244**.1-2
  child marriage **202**.19; **244**.15; **248**.24-5
  and civil partnerships **225**.35
  common law marriage **244**.8-9
  ending *see* divorce
  financial incentives **191**.2
  forced marriages **224**.3, 14-15, 36-7; **244**.3, 12-14
    and Islam **215**.12
  history of **244**.4-5, 8-9
  and Islam **215**.12
  and law **244**.1-3, 5, 8-9
  same-sex couples **225**.33; **244**.16-29
  statistics **191**.1, 3
  and stepfamilies *see* stepfamilies
  and transsexuals **225**.27
  trends **191**.1-4
Marriage Act 1753 **244**.9
Marriage Foundation **244**.11
Marriage (Same-sex Couples) Bill **244**.19-20
maternal (metaphase) spindle transfer **247**.29, 31
maternity leave **183**.18, 21, 23, 24; **191**.37-8
  effect on businesses **183**.23
maternity pay **191**.38
maternity rights **191**.37-8
maturity as a factor in sentencing young people **223**.33-4

MBCT (mindfulness-based cognitive therapy) **190**.34-6
mealtimes and recovering anorexics **249**.37
meat consumption
  bushmeat trade **193**.23
  meat substitutes **214**.9, 11
  need to reduce **214**.15-16, 22-3, 24, 27
  nutrients **205**.3; **214**.34-5
  red meat and health **214**.34-5
meat free foods **214**.7-8
Meat Free Mondays campaign **214**.27
meat production
  arguments for and against **214**.18-21
  from cloned cows **211**.12, 15-17
  and the environment **214**.16, 17, 18-19, 20-21
  intensively farming **233**.3, 7-8
  laboratory-grown meat **211**.20-21
  large-scale pig farms **233**.11
  product labelling rules **205**.11
  sustainable **214**.14, 20-21, 23
media **210**.1-39
  and body image **234**.5, 7, 8, 10, 11, 18
  and celebrities as role models **238**.13
  climate change reporting **216**.22-4
  drug death reporting **186**.32-3
  and eating disorders **249**.15, 25-31
  employment of ethnic minorities **236**.11
  and gambling **203**.26
  influence on young people smoking **188**.25-6
  and Islamophobia **215**.33; **236**.23-4
  and mental ill health **201**.23
  multi-tasking **210**.11
  new technologies **210**.13-26
  and the permissive society **196**.25-6
  and privacy **210**.33-9
  public opinion on media freedom **229**.12
  regulation **210**.27-9, 34
  and religion **215**.13
  representation of young people **239**.6
  and Scottish Gypsy Travellers **236**.22
  and sexualisation of children **238**.3, 13, 32-3
  and suicide **199**.35, 36
  trends **210**.1-12
  violence *see* violence, media
  WikiLeaks **210**.20-26
  see also broadcasters; films; Internet; magazines; newspapers; press; radio; telecommunications; television
medical abortion **231**.7
medical ethics argument against euthanasia **217**.4
medical insurance **251**.5-6
  and use of NHS **251**.7
medical model of disability **197**.2
medical profession
  and assisted suicide **217**.22, 24-5
  effects of legalizing assisted dying **217**.4, 8, 11, 31
  see also doctors
medical research, use of animals **233**.28-39
medical treatment
  injured service personnel **213**.2, 8-9, 10-11
  patient's right to refuse **217**.13, 25
  withdrawing **217**.14

see also palliative care

medically-assisted dying *see* physician-assisted suicide

medicinal drug use, cannabis **186**.8, 16-17

medicines
    consumer buying habits **195**.8
      Internet purchasing **195**.8, 39
    from GM plants **208**.21-2
    from GM animals **208**.13
    labelling of additives **205**.16
    and obesity **241**.16
    for stress and anxiety **206**.3, 13
    see also drug treatments; drugs

meditation as treatment for depression **190**.34-6; **195**.15

mega-farms **233**.9-11

Megan's Law **248**.35

Members of Parliament *see* MPs

memorial websites **192**.38-9

memories of the deceased *see* remembrance of the deceased

men
    and abortion **231**.9
    and alcohol limits **194**.14
    body image concerns **234**.13, 16-17
    career aspirations **221**.21
    and compulsive shopping **207**.6
    as domestic abuse victims **224**.5, 9-10, 11
    and eating disorders **249**.3, 4-5, 15, 18-19
    fertility
      and age **247**.6
      fertility drugs **247**.9
      problems **247**.2
    and household tasks **221**.6
    and HPV vaccine **237**.27
    Internet usage **230**.3-4
    and IVF procedure **247**.10
    media usage **210**.12
    and mental health problems **190**.18-19
    parenting roles **191**.30-33
    paternity leave **221**.4-5
    paternity rights **191**.39
    post-natal depression **190**.16-17
    and prostitution **246**.24-5
    and sexually transmitted infections **237**.19, 22
    and smoking **188**.1, 15
    and suicide **199**.21, 28
    symptoms of stress **206**.7-8
    as victims of trafficking **246**.39
    see also boys and young men; fathers; gay men

Mencap **197**.39

Mendel, Gregor **211**.2

Mental Capacity Act and right to refuse medical treatment **217**.13

mental health **252**.13-26
    and abortion **231**.14-15
    and alcohol **194**.6
    benefits of exercise **241**.4, 33-4
    and body image **234**.10, 11, 19
    and cannabis **186**.10-13, 16, 28-9, 30, 31, 32; **228**.8
    children, and aggression **224**.23
    definition **201**.33, 35

and homeless people **189**.9-11
    improving **201**.33-4, 35-6
    statistics, young people **190**.27; **252**.2
    and stress **206**.36-7
    strategies **201**.5, 35
    students **185**.8
    young people **190**.27; **252**.2, 13-26
    see also dementia; depression

Mental Health Act **201**.38-9
    'nearest relative' powers **190**.11

mental health services **201**.5
    insufficiencies **201**.37
    and young people **201**.10-11, 36

mental illness **201**.1-39
    and Armed Forces personnel **213**.3-4, 5, 6
    attitudes to **201**.22-3, 31
    and cannabis **228**.8
    causes **201**.32-3
    children **201**.2-4
    costs **201**.1, 23
    and domestic violence **224**.7
    ex-service personnel **213**.33-4
    and gambling **203**.37
    and homosexuality **201**.3
    prevalence **201**.5, 6
    and self-harm **199**.2
    and social welfare problems **201**.29
    stigma **201**.22-3, 31
      self-stigma **201**.28
      young carers **201**.8
    and suicide **199**.21, 24
    young people **201**.2-4, 7, 29-30
    see also bipolar affective disorder; dementia; depression; post-traumatic stress disorder; schizophrenia

mental symptoms
    of anxiety **206**.10
    of stress **206**.1-2, 9, 19

mentoring
    of girls **221**.32
    of young people by ex-service personnel **213**.32

mephedrone (meow meow) **228**.23, 36, 37
    classification **228**.21-2, 23, 32
    deaths **252**.32

mercy killing *see* non-voluntary euthanasia

metabolic syndrome and vegetarianism **214**.31-2

metabolically healthy obese people **241**.17

metal waste exports, EU **242**.18

metaphase (maternal) spindle transfer **247**.29, 31

methamphetamine (crystal meth) **228**.23

methane
    as car fuel **204**.39
    emissions from biodegradable products **218**.37

methcathinones **252**.32

Methodist Church and abortion **231**.19

methoxetamine (MXE/Mexxy) **228**.6

metro systems **200**.34

Metropolitan Police and racism **236**.26
    and herbal medicine registration (THR) **195**.4, 35, 38

microdosing as alternative to animal research **233**.32

microfinance **235**.34-5

microgeneration of energy **204**.35-6
    solar water heating **204**.21-2
    water power **204**.19
Mid-Staffordshire NHS Foundation Trust public inquiry **251**.3, 4, 14-15, 16
middle-classes **219**.1-2, 9-10
Middle East
    child soldiers **202**.33
    criminalization of homosexuality **225**.39
    press freedom **196**.2
    as tourist destination **222**.8
middle-income countries **235**.28-30
Middleton, Kate **232**.5-6
midwives, religious objection to abortion **231**.30
MIGA (Multilateral Investment Guarantee Agency) **226**.10
migrant families and child abuse **248**.22-3
migrant workers **220**.32-3
    East European, racism towards **236**.32
    integration **236**.17
    returning due to unemployment **220**.34
    women **220**.35
migration **220**.8-9, 20-39
    and climate change **220**.38, 39
    elimination of barriers, economic benefits **226**.39
    forced **220**.36-7
    and population growth **220**.9
    reasons for **220**.20, 36-7
    statistics **220**.21
    to UK **220**.20-21, 24-5
    of workforce (brain drain) **220**.32-3
    see also asylum seekers; immigration
mild cognitive impairment **239**.29
military forces, USA, and sexual orientation **225**.38-9
Military to Mentors programme **213**.32
milk
    from cloned cows **211**.12, 13-14
    and balanced diet **205**.3, 28
    labelling of milk products **205**.11
Millennium Development Goals **226**.3; 1-2, 25-7
    2011 report **218**.39
    education **229**.27-8
    employment **235**.26
    hunger **235**.26-7
    poverty reduction **235**.25-6
    water and sanitation **218**.31, 36-7
Mind **241**.12
mindfulness-based cognitive therapy (MBCT) **190**.34-6
mini pill (contraception) **237**.6
minimum income standard **235**.3, 5
minimum pricing, alcohol **194**.36, 37
minimum wage, young workers **183**.28
Ministers, government **240**.26
minority ethnic groups see ethnic minorities
minority rights **229**.24-39
Miras (mortgage interest tax relief) **253**.17
miscarriage and IVF **247**.7
missing children **248**.28
Misuse of Drugs Act 1971 **228**.21, 22, 24
    sentencing guidelines **228**.28-31
mitochondrial diseases prevented by three-parent

IVF **247**.29-34
MNCs see (multi-national corporations)
mobile phones
    and blogging **210**.16
    bullying by **232**.17, 25, 27, 29
    and Internet access **230**.1
    and pornography access by children and young people **238**.4, 19; **246**.11
    and relationship abuse **224**.20
    sexting **238**.23-4
    and social networking **210**.14
    usage trends **210**.11
        and gender **210**.12
        international comparison **210**.13-14
mockery as indirect racism **236**.28
Modafinil **252**.33, 34
modeling
    agencies targeting eating disorder sufferers **249**.26
    model dies of anorexia **234**.36
    and sexualisation of children **238**.27-8
    teenagers **234**.35; **238**.38
models of disability **197**.2
monarchy, UK **240**.22-3
    arguments against **240**.24-5
money
    money management see financial skills
    students see students and money matters
    see also banks; credit; debt; incomes; wages
money worries
    children **250**.20
    and depression **190**.5
    and health **250**.29, 33
    and stress **206**.18, 21, 39
Mongolia, education programme **229**.28
Monitor (NHS regulator) **251**.25-6, 31
monoamine oxidase inhibitors (MAOIs) **190**.11, 33
mood stabilising drugs **190**.10
moral rights of embryos **211**.31, 34
morality and business **227**.22-3
morning after pill see emergency contraception
mortality
    Armed Forces mortality rate **213**.9
    and depression **190**.20
    and population trends **220**.9
    see also deaths; life expectancy
mortgage interest tax relief (Miras) **253**.17
motherhood role and the abortion debate **231**.18-19
mothers
    in the Army **213**.13-14
    girl soldiers **202**.36
    HIV transmission to children **243**.1-2, 25
    maternity rights **191**.37-8
    as migrant workers **220**.35
    and pay gap **221**.24
    preferring not to work **183**.25
    stay-at-home mothers suffering stress **191**.35
    see also working mothers
motoring
    and disability **197**.11
    see also cars; driving
motorways
    M4 bus lane **200**.36

motorway phobia **200**.4

motorway travel frequency **200**.5

mourning *see* grief

movies *see* films

MPs

and the drugs debate **186**.34-5

ethnic minority **236**.11

female **221**.13, 15, 20

MRI (magnetic resonance imaging) as alternative to animal research **233**.32

Muamba, Fabrice, subject of Twitter racism **236**.31

Multilateral Investment Guarantee Agency (MIGA) **226**.10

multinational corporations (MNCs) **226**.1, 27

and tax **227**.32-3

multiple births and fertility treatment **247**.4

multiple sclerosis (MS)

classification as disability **197**.1

stem cell treatment **211**.38-9

Munro Review **248**.1 muscular dystrophies **197**.3

muscle dysmorphic disorder (bigorexia) **249**.7

musculoskeletal health and physical activity **241**.4-5

music videos

age ratings **238**.5

sexual content **238**.20-22

Muslims

anti-Muslim hate crime **215**.28-30; **236**.14, 24

British **215**.9-12; **240**.17-18

discrimination against **215**.30, 31-2

media portrayal **236**.23-4

Muslim extremists, protests against British soldiers **196**.9-10

public attitudes to **212**.4, 30-31; **215**.33

ritual slaughter **233**.16

as stop and search targets **212**.28-9

veiling of Muslim women **215**.34-8

see also Islam; Islamophobia

MXE (methoxetamine) **228**.6

My Money Week education project **250**.17

Myanmar, forced labour **229**.15

MySpace, reporting inappropriate content **232**.35

N

NAMA (non-agricultural market access) **226**.15-16

name-calling, dealing with **232**.19-20

nanotechnology **208**.15-16

National Assembly for Wales **240**.27

National Child Measurement Programme **241**.24

National Citizen Service programme **240**.33-4

National Commissioning Board (NHS) **251**.25

National Crime Agency **223**.22

National DNA Database **245**.14-15

National Health Service *see* NHS

national identity

British *see* British identity

National Institute for Clinical Excellence (NICE) *see* NICE

National Insurance **250**.15

National Lottery

disability sports funding **198**.18

online participation **203**.4

national origins

of UK population **240**.15-16

natural family planning **182**.19

natural gas, industry trends **204**.1

natural resources consumption **218**.7-8, 13-14

impact of global development **226**.3-4

impact of tourism **222**.29

water **218**.33

Nazareth, Colombia, ban on tourists **222**.32

NCDL (National Canine Defence League) **233**.1

nearest relative under Mental Health Act **190**.11; **201**.38-9

needle sharing and HIV transmission **243**.1

NEETs (young people not in employment, education or training) **183**.32; **252**.21

negative body image see body image, negative

neglect **248**.3, 14-20

law reform **248**.35

trafficked children **202**.29

Netherlands, The

assisted dying legislation **217**.2, 9, 11

elderly people's fears of euthanasia **217**.33

health care **251**.9

LGBT equality policy **225**.13

sex education **182**.28-9, 32-4; **237**.33-4

neurobiology and sexual orientation **225**.15-16

New Deal **183**.29

New Horizons programme (NHS) **251**.3

New Strategic Direction for Alcohol and Drugs (N.Ireland) **228**.24

news media and women **210**.6-8

female presenters and reporters **210**.7

women as news subjects **210**.6, 7-8

News of the World, phone-hacking **210**.35-6

newspapers **210**.1-2

display of sexualized images **238**.5

ownership **210**.2

paid-for websites **210**.19

regulations **210**.27-8

NGOs (non-governmental organisations) **226**.1, 4

NHS (National Health Service) **219**.12; **251**.1-10

age discrimination ban **239**.11

anti-smoking strategies, pregnant women **188**.30-32

constitution **251**.3, 4, 27-8

costs of overweight and obesity **241**.3

costs of smoking **188**.22

disability discrimination **197**.30, 38-9

funding **251**.1, 36

funding crisis **251**.34-5, 38

public opinions **251**.20-21

and herbal medicine **195**.11

history **251**.2-4

and homeopathy **195**.16, 17-22, 24-5

international comparisons **251**.8, 9

and IVF treatment **247**.10, 22-5

open data policy **245**.12-13

patients with learning difficulties **197**.38-9

post traumatic stress disorder treatment **213**.3-4

public opinions **251**.19-22

quality of care **251**.8, 11-13, 33

reform **251**.25-39

self-harm treatment **199**.13-14, 15, 18

size **251**.1
staff survey **251**.18
structure **251**.1, 4, 25-6, 29, 30-32
NHS and Community Care Act **251**.3
NHS Direct **251**.3
NHS England **251**.4, 30
NICE (National Institute for Clinical Excellence)
251.26
drink-driving study **194**.32
guidelines on IVF **247**.10, 22-5, 27
guidelines on reducing alcohol-related harm
194.33, 36-8
nicotine
addiction **188**.10, 16
effects on heart **188**.7
poisoning, tobacco pickers **188**.39
nicotine replacement therapies **188**.6
VAT on **188**.23
night eating syndrome **249**.8
night shelters *see* hostels for homeless people
Nimrod aircraft contract cancellation **213**.21
niqab, arguments for and against wearing **215**.37-8
nocturnal sleep-related eating disorder **249**.8
noise
from traffic **200**.14-15, 22
from wind turbines **204**.12
non-agricultural market access (NAMA) **226**.15-16
non-governmental organisations (NGOs) **226**.1, 4
non-native species, impact of **193**.12
UK **193**.38-9
non-reproductive cloning *see* therapeutic cloning
non-voluntary euthanasia **217**.5
Kay Inglis **217**.27, 29
Nordic countries, criminality of prostitution **246**.20
North Korea, death penalty **229**.37
North London Cares **239**.38
Northern Ireland
abortion law **231**.3, 25
drug strategy **228**.24
homelessness **189**.4
and national identity **240**.12
Northern Ireland Assembly **240**.27
Republican terrorist groups **212**.14
young people's sexual lifestyles **237**.15-17
Norway, exporting waste to Sweden **242**.37
novel foods **211**.17
Novel Foods Regulation and clonng **211**.12
novel psychoactive substances *see* legal high drugs
NSPCC **252**.15
How safe are our children? report **248**.7
report on children missing from care homes
248.28
nuclear power **204**.26
political support for **216**.25
nurses giving sex education lessons **237**.34
nutrition
and food groups **205**.2-3, 4-5
and GM crops **208**.35-6
and meat **214**.34-5
nutrition labelling **205**.13
organic produce **205**.36
Quorn products **214**.9
and veganism **214**.3

and vegetarianism **214**.28-39
see also diet; healthy eating

O

Obama, Barack, and closure of Guantánamo Bay
212.33, 34-5
obesity and overweight **205**.19-21; **241**.2-3, 14-24
and alcohol **194**.18
avoidance *see* weight management
causes **241**.15-16
in children *see* childhood obesity
government strategies **205**.20-21
and health **241**.15, 17
and life expectancy **241**.15
statistics **241**.2-3, 15
treatment costs **241**.3, 18-19
and young people **252**.2
see also body weight; weight management
Obscene Publications Acts **196**.14, 22; **246**.7
oceans
acidification **193**.30
threats to **218**.24-5
occupational pensions **250**.12
occupational segregation **221**.19, 27-9
occupational therapists **197**.4
Ofcom **196**.18-20
Broadcasting Code **210**.27
and offensive language on television **196**.21, 24
Offences against the Person Act 1861 **231**.1
Offender Discrimination Act **223**.27
offenders
recovery programmes **223**.23-4
and restorative justice **223**.28-9
see also ex-offenders
offensive language
and disabled people **197**.28-9
on television **196**.21, 24
offensive material
broadcasters' rights **196**.24
cartoons in airport prayer room **196**.11-12
offsetting carbon *see* carbon offsetting
offshore wind power **204**.14-18
Ofsted and sexuality equality legislation **225**.7
OHSS (ovarian hyper-stimulation syndrome) **247**.7
oil
arguments against production **204**.9-10
industry trends **204**.1
older people
abuse of **224**.4; **239**.4, 34
as an asset **239**.16
care *see* care services for older people
communications trends **210**.11-12
and dementia *see* dementia
and HIV /AIDS **243**.18-19
and health **239**.4, 8, 10, 24-39
health benefits of dance **241**.33-4
hospital care **251**.11-13
in employment *see* older workers
Internet usage **230**.5, 19-21
lesbian, gay and bisexual people **239**.10

physical activity recommendations **241**.6
and poverty **235**.6, 8; **239**.8, 17, 18
shared ownership housing scheme **253**.8
and suicide **199**.20, 21
wellbeing **239**.8-9, 13
see also age discrimination; ageing population; grandparents
older women and IVF **247**.10, 22-6
older workers **183**.15, 27; **239**.16, 18
Olympic Games
foreign-born athletes in Team GB **240**.10-11
gender equality **198**.19
London, opening ceremony, use of animals **233**.13
and pride in Britain **240**.9
and sex trafficking **229**.20
sporting legacy **241**.9, 10
and sports competition for young people **198**.5
talent identification **198**.8-10
and tourist industry **222**.12-13
see also Paralympic Games
omega 3 fatty acids **214**.29, 33
one-parent families *see* lone parents
online bullying *see* cyberbullying
online divorce services **244**.34, 35
online gambling **203**.28-9
participation rates **203**.4
women **203**.35-6
young people **203**.16-18
online grooming **230**.23-4
online personal data
children's **245**.16
consumer awareness **245**.17-19
protection **245**.20
and risk of fraud **245**.21-2
online racism **236**.31
online reputation **230**.31-2
online retail *see* Internet shopping
online safety *see* safety and the Internet
online socialising *see* social networking
online travel booking **222**.3
open data policy **245**.12-13
oral sex and safety **237**.3
Oregon State, assisted dying legislation **217**.2, 11
organ donation **192**.28
from euthanasia victims **217**.32
Organ Donation Register **251**.3
organ harvesting and human trafficking **229**.18
organ transplants *see* therapeutic cloning
organic farming
and the environment **205**.34, 35
and food safety **205**.34, 36
organic food **205**.30, 33, 34-6; **214**.23, 29
arguments against **205**.34
arguments for **205**.35-6
consumer attitudes **207**.30
organic waste
energy generation **204**.6
gas production **204**.24
Origin Assured fur assurance scheme **233**.19
orthorexia nervosa **249**.8
osteoarthritis **239**.26; **241**.4-5
osteoporosis **239**.26; **241**.4-5

and cannabis use **186**.6
effect of salt intake **205**.25-6
outsourcing of Internet control **196**.33-4
ovarian hyper-stimulation syndrome (OHSS) **247**.7
overall poverty **235**.1
overdoses *see* drug overdoses
overseas adoption **247**.15, 17
overseas burial **192**.31
overseas surrogacy arrangements **247**.19
overseas travel, attitudes to **222**.2
see also tourism
overweight people   *see* obesity and overweight
ovo-vegetarians **214**.2
ovulation problems **247**.1
and fertility drugs **247**.8-9
ownership, newspapers **210**.2
Oxbridge
entrance tests **185**.23
teachers' misconceptions about **185**.24
Oxford child trafficking case **246**.37

P

Pacific Ocean, marine debris **242**.21
packed lunches, children **205**.7, 10
pain and depression **239**.32
pain relief
and cannabis **186**.16
and the placebo effect **195**.28-9
see also palliative care
palliative care **217**.10, 15-17, 18, 38
and assisted dying **217**.11, 17
availability **217**.15-16
effectiveness **217**.16
limitations **217**.10, 11, 16
Scotland **217**.18
palliative sedation **217**.3, 14, 25
palm oil industry and biodiversity **193**.8-9
pancreatitis **194**.6
panic attacks **206**.11, 16
Papadopoulos, Dr Linda (psychologist) **238**.10-12
paper layer of privacy **245**.2-3
Paralympic Games **198**.20
talent identification **198**.22
parental leave **183**.18, 22, 24, 27; **191**.34, 39; **221**.4-5, 24
for adoption **247**.16
parental orders and surrogacy **247**.19
parental relationships
effect on children **191**.1
and youth homelessness **189**.27
parental separation
effect on children **191**.1, 9; **244**.36-7
online help **244**.34
parenting orders **223**.32
parents
and adult children **191**.26-8
and alcohol
alcohol abuse **194**.27-8
influence on children's drinking **194**.25-6
attitudes to school learning styles **209**.1-3

and children's aggression **224**.22-3
and children's body image **234**.10
and children's education attainment **219**.26, 27, 33
and children's gambling **203**.13
and children's Internet activity **238**.5, 25; **246**.15; **245**.26-7
and children's obesity **241**.20, 23
death of a child **192**.20-23
empty nest syndrome disproved **191**.29
health advice source for young people **252**.4-5
of lesbians and gays **225**.3-4
with mental health problems, effects on children **201**.4, 8-9
parenting styles **191**.5
influence on children's character **191**.191.6
in prison, effects on children **201**.4
putting pressure on schools **209**.4
satisfaction with schools **209**.21
and sexualisation of children
concerns about **238**.7, 10, 14, 20, 35
encouraging **238**.36-7
of sexually exploited children **202**.23; **248**.31
sex education role **182**.34-5
smoking, influence on young people smoking **188**.28
and stress
long working hours **206**.22-3
stay-at-home parents **191**.35
and student finance **250**.24
support for children's education **209**.36
supporting adult children **191**.26-8
teaching financial skills **250**.21
and teenage depression **190**.27
using pension to help children buy homes **253**.17
young parents **182**.14-18
see also divorce; families; fathers; lone parents; mothers; working parents
Paris, cycle hire **200**.31
Parkinson's disease and animal research **233**.36, 38
parks, fitness equipment **241**.36-7
Parliament **240**.3, 25
ethnic minority members **236**.11
Scottish **240**.27
women members **221**.13, 15, 20, 37
part-time jobs
and the gender pay gap **221**.24, 28
students **209**.32
parties, political *see* political parties
passive euthanasia **217**.5
passive smoking **188**.5, 10-11, 12
children **252**.38
passive victims of bullying **232**.8
pasteurization **211**.2
patents on GM seeds **208**.3-4
paternity leave **183**.18, 22, 24; **191**.34-5, 39; **221**.4-5
pathological gambling *see* problem gambling
patients
elderly patients' care **251**.11-13
rights to choice **251**.3, 26
rights to refuse treatment **217**.13, 25
patriotic hacking **196**.34-5

patriotism and the Union Jack **240**.4-5
pay gap
ethnic **236**.18
gender **221**.22-5, 27-8, 35-6, 37
payday loans **235**.11; **250**.5, 6
PAYE (Pay As You Earn) **250**.13
payment methods trends **250**.3
PBRM1 gene and depression **190**.12-13
PCC *see* Press Complaints Commission
PCOS (polycystic ovary syndrome) **247**.1
peace negotiations, female participation **221**.37
peer mentoring, young parents **182**.39
peer pressure and drinking behaviour **194**.12
peer support
for eating disorders **249**.20
and suicide **199**.33
pelvic inflammatory disease **247**.2
penalties
cannabis supply **186**.2, 30
possession of cannabis **186**.1-2, 5, 9, 30
pensions **239**.15, 19
Army **213**.2
claiming after a death **192**.32-3
saving for **239**.14; **250**.36
workplace pensions **250**.12
people smuggling **229**.18; **246**.30
periods, sex during **237**.3, 11
permissive behaviour, effect of the media **196**.25-6
Perry pre-school programme **219**.35
personal information **245**.11-27
children's data held without parental consent **245**.16
consumer concerns about online data **245**.17-19
control of **230**.24, 30
and Data Protection Act **245**.11
protecting **245**.20
and risk of fraud **245**.21-2
Personal, Social, Health and Economic (PSHE) education
covering sexualisation and gender stereotyping **238**.4, 11, 14
personalization of care **197**.13
pescetarian diet **214**.1
pest control and animal welfare **233**.4
pesticides
and GM crops **208**.3, 21, 23
and organic farming **205**.34, 35-6
Petermann Glacier **216**.15
pets, exotic
demand for, impact on biodiversity in Asia **193**.20-21
impact on British wildlife **193**.39
pharmaceutical industry and GM crops **208**.21-2
pharmaceutical waste and water pollution **218**.38-9
phenazepam **228**.25
philanthropy **227**.20-21
Philippines, horse fighting **233**.27
philosophical beliefs, Equality Act definition **215**.24
phishing **230**.30
phobias **206**.11
in children **206**.13
treatment **206**.12-13
phone-hacking **210**.35-6

Photoshopping *see* airbrushing
physical abuse
    of children **248**.3
    as domestic abuse **224**.1, 3
    of trafficked children **202**.29
physical activity *see* exercise
physical disabilities **197**.3-5
physician-assisted suicide (PAS)
    doctors' opposition to **217**.22
    prevalence **217**.24-5
    see also assisted suicide
physiotherapists **197**.4
phytoplankton **193**.5
pica **249**.8
Pick's disease **201**.10
pig farming, mega-farms **233**.10-11
Pilkington, Lesley **225**.17
pill, contraceptive **182**.19; **237**.6-7
    over the counter availability **182**.21-3
PIPA (Protect IP Act) **230**.35-6, 37
pipe smoking **188**.3
piracy on the Internet **230**.35-6
placebo effect **195**.28-9
    and homeopathy **195**.26, 27, 29
planning laws and inequality **218**.3, 4
planning permission reform **253**.27
plastic bags **242**.25-7
    used in road surfacing **242**.28
Plastic Brits (foreign-born athletes) **240**.10-11
plastic surgery *see* cosmetic surgery
plastic waste
    broken down by fungus **242**.27
    import ban by China **242**.21
    in Pacific Ocean **242**.21
    plastic bags **242**.25-7, 28
    recycling **242**.23, 24
Platform 51 **221**.28
play and disabled children **197**.37
pluripotent stem cells **211**.28, 35-7
    see also embryonic stem cells; iPS cells
pocket money **250**.39
poisoning, emergency treatment **199**.14
poker, online **203**.28-9
police
    drug classification, effects on policing **186**.36-7
    open data policy **245**.12
    and racism **236**.10, 26-7
    reporting a crime **223**.12
    reporting sexual assault **237**.13-14
    and Terrorism Act **212**.16
Policing and Crime Act and prostitution **246**.17, 18-19
political correctness verdus free speech **236**.35-7
political debates, inclusion of the BNP **196**.7, 8
political material, Ofcom regulation **196**.19
political parties, views on climate change **216**.25
politics
    and middle classes **219**.10
    recent British politics **240**.21
    women's participation **221**.2, 13, 15, 20, 37
    women's right to vote **221**.36
    young people's involvement **240**.39
        and the Internet **230**.9

    see also government; MPs; Parliament; voting
pollinating insects, declining numbers **193**.27-8
pollution
    effects on wildlife **193**.2
    see also emissions; water pollution
polonium-210 in cigarette smoke **188**.9
polycystic ovary syndrome (PCOS) **247**.1
polygamy **244**.3, 4
    and Islam **215**.12
pools **203**.4
Poor Laws **219**.11
poorism (slum tourism) **222**.16, 33-4
POP (progestogen only pill) **237**.6-7
pop-culture tourism **222**.16
population *see* ageing population; population growth
population growth **218**.26-30; **220**.1-15
    controlling **218**.26-7; **220**.4, 10, 16-17, 19
    developed countries **220**.1
    developing countries **220**.2, 4
    economic effects **220**.7
    effects **220**.4, 5-7
    and the environment **220**.4, 6-7, 14
    and food supply **218**.29-30; 3-4, 6
    growth rate **220**.1-2, 3, 13
    projections **220**.2, 8-9
    statistics **220**.4
    and sustainability **218**.5
    UK **220**.19
pornography **246**.1-16
    and children and young people **246**.10-11, 12
    education about **246**.12-13, 14
    effects **238**.16-26; **246**.1-2, 10-11, 12, 13
    and the Internet **202**.18; **238**.16, 19, 25, 26; **246**.3
        children viewing **196**.38; **238**.3-4, 14-15;
246.10-   11
        filters **246**.7-8, 15-16
        women viewing **230**.2-3
    and lads' magazines **238**.18
    and the law **246**.7-8, 9
    and mobile phones **238**.4, 19
    and prostitution **246**.24
    and women's choices **246**.3, 4-5
    see also child pornography
pornography industry **246**.11
    and women **246**.3, 4-5
    regulation, LA County **246**.5
porpoises, impact of climate change **193**.29
Portman Group **194**.39
Portugal, decriminalisation of drugs possession **228**.34
positive action and age discrimination **239**.13
possession of drugs
    cannabis **186**.1-2, 5, 9, 30; **228**.28-9
    sentencing guidelines **228**.28-31
post-2015 development framework and child protection **248**.32-3
post-compulsory education
    see A-levels; higher education; universities
post-mortem, hospital **192**.31
post-natal depression **190**.2, 14-17, 21-2
    fathers **190**.16-17
    mothers **190**.16-17

and suicide risk **190**.24

  symptoms of **190**.14

post-traumatic stress disorder (PTSD) **201**.20-21

  service personnel **213**.3-4, 5

  therapies **213**.34

postgraduate destinations **185**.32

postgraduate study **185**.30

potatoes

  genetically modified **208**.11

  powering batteries **204**.39

poverty

  and child labour **202**.4

  and child trafficking **202**.27

  children living in *see* child poverty

  and children's wellbeing **191**.9

  definitions **235**.1, 2-3

  and disabled people **197**.35; **235**.5, 7

  and education **209**.13-14, 34-5; **235**.21-2

    pupil premium **209**.18

  and free trade **226**.14, 29-30, 33

  fuel poverty *see* fuel poverty

  and girl's schooling **221**.39

  global **226**.17; **235**.23-39

  lone parent families **191**.1

  and mental health problems **201**.4

  and Millennium Development Goals **218**.39; **235**.1-
    2, 25-7

  and older people **235**.6, 8; **239**.8, 17, 18

  and population growth **220**.6

  reduction

    through migration **226**.39

    through trade **226**.28

  rich-poor gap, UK **235**.12, 13

    and sport participation **241**.29

  statistics **235**.5-8, 23, 24

  and transport, developing countries **200**.13

  in the UK **235**.1-22

  and women **221**.34

  see also child poverty; inequality

poverty cycle **235**.35

poverty tourism **222**.16, 33-4

power and control wheel **224**.7

power stations using biomass **204**.5, 7

Prader-Willi Syndrome **249**.8

Pratchett, Terry, assisted suicide documentary **217**.20

pre-implantation genetic testing **247**.8

pre-marital doubts and risk of divorce **244**.32-3

pregnancy **182**.3-5; **247**.1

  and alcohol **194**.14

  and dietary supplements **205**.4

  and domestic abuse **224**.4-5

    effects on unborn babies **224**.24, 37

  and eating disorders **249**.12

  employment rights **191**.37-8

  and HIV diagnosis **243**.13

  and HIV transmission to baby **243**.1-2, 25

  myths about getting pregnant **237**.3, 4, 11, 35

  pregnancy options counselling **231**.36-7

  risks **182**.11, 37

  and school **182**.6

  and sex education **237**.8

  and smoking **188**.11, 31

  NHS anti-smoking strategies **188**.30-32

  testing **182**.4-5

  unplanned, statistics **237**.9-10

  your choices **182**.6, 8-9

  see also abortion; teenage pregnancies

prejudice

  Islamaphobia *see* Islamophobia

  against working classes **219**.3-4, 5-6

  see also discrimination; homophobia; racial prejudice

premature babies, survival rate **231**.21, 22

prescription charges introduction **251**.2

presenteeism **183**.9

press

  press freedom, global study **196**.1-2

  press self-regulation, public support for **196**.6

  Youth Parliament manifesto **240**.39

  see also media

Press Complaints Commission **196**.3, 4-5

  Editor's Code **210**.27-8

  reform proposals **210**.29

  statement on phone-hacking **210**.36

Pretty, Diane **217**.1-2, 24

Prevent strategy (anti-terrorism) **212**.17-18

Prevention of Cruelty to Children Acts **248**.35

Prevention of Terrorism Act 2005 **212**.19

price of alcohol **194**.35

  minimum pricing **194**.36, 37

pricing

  Fairtrade prices **226**.36

  misleading practices **207**.15

Primark and sexualised clothes for children **238**.31

Primary Care Trusts (PCTs) **251**.3

  abolition **251**.25

primates, endangered species **193**.22-3

Prime Minister **240**.26

prison

  and ex-service personnel **213**.4, 36, 37-9

  and the Human Rights Act **229**.5, 6

  and mental health, young people **201**.4

  prison leavers and homelessness **189**.6

  prison sentences **223**.19-20, 21

    not a deterrent for knife crime **223**.34

  prisoners' right to vote **229**.35-6

  suicide rate **199**.25

  women prisoners and self-harm **199**.12

  and work **223**.23

  and young people **223**.28-9

  see also youth custody

privacy **245**.1-39

  history of **245**.2-4

  Human Rights Act **196**.38; **245**.1

  and the law **245**.1-10

  and the media **210**.28, 33-9

    Human Rights Act **229**.5

  online **232**.28; **245**.3, 16-27

  and social networking **210**.33-4; **230**.33-4

  see also freedom of information; personal information

Privacy and Electronic Communications Regulations **245**.9

private life, right to **245**.1

private medical insurance **251**.5-6

patients using NHS **251**.7

private schools and children with learning problems **197**.15

Privy Council **240**.22

pro-abortion (pro-choice) arguments **231**.1, 16

pro-eating disorder websites **249**.29-31

pro-life arguments **231**.1, 16

problem drinking *see* alcohol abuse

problem gambling **203**.2, 6, 19-39

    causes **203**.19

    children **203**.12, 15

    definition **203**.6, 12, 19

    genetic link **203**.30-31

    help **203**.21, 24-5, 34, 36

    Internet gambling **203**.28-9, 35-6

    people at risk **203**.23

    prevalence **203**.20

    signs **203**.2, 23

    social context **203**.32-3

    treatment **203**.24-5, 27

    women **203**.26, 35-6

    young people **203**.9-10, 11, 12, 15, 16

Proceeds of Crime Act and sex workers **246**.23

professions and social mobility **185**.38-9

progestogen only pill (mini pill) **237**.6-7

Project HE:RO (Health Engagement: Real Outcomes) **241**.35

pronuclear transfer method, three-parent IVF **247**.29, 31

property crime **223**.4

property rights, disabled people **197**.21-2

proportional representation systems **240**.29

proscribed organizations **212**.15-16, 19

    Islamic **212**.10

prostitution **246**.17-29

    advice for sex workers **246**.21-3

    deterrents **246**.24-5

    children **202**.17, 24-6

    effects on society **246**.19-20

    government policies **246**.17-18

    and the law **246**.17, 18-19, 21-3, 28

    legalisation debate **246**.20, 26

    men's attitudes to **246**.24-5

    reasons for using **246**.25

    and sex trafficking **229**.19-20; **246**.29, 33

    statistics **246**.19

Protection of Animals Act 1911 **233**.1-2

Protection of Children Act **248**.35

    and film classification **196**.14

Protection of Freedoms Act and CCTV **245**.32

proteins **214**.34

    and mental health **252**.25

    and vegetarian diet **214**.12, 29, 30, 33

provocative victims of bullying **232**.8

Przewalski's horse **233**.26

PSHE (Personal, Social, Health and Economic) education

    covering sexualisation and gender stereotyping **238**.4, 11, 14

psycho-social causes of homosexuality **225**.2

psychological abuse as domestic abuse **224**.3

psychological effects

    of cannabis **186**.7-8, 9-13, 16, 28-9, 30, 31, 32

    of human cloning **211**.27

on trafficked children **202**.29

psychosis **201**.18-19

    and cannabis use **186**.10, 12, 13, 31, 32

psychotherapy

    and depression **190**.5, 11, 34

    lack of availability **190**.37

psychotic depression **190**.2

PTSD *see* post-traumatic stress disorder)

puberty and anorexia **249**.2, 17

pubic lice (crabs) **237**.21

public access to crime data **223**.1-2

public appointments, women **221**.14, 15

public attitudes

    to assisted suicide **217**.23, 34

    to biodiversity **216**.11; **218**.17

    to biotechnology **211**.5-6

    to burqa wearing **215**.39

    to business **227**.11, 13-14

    to CCTV **245**.28, 29

    to climate change **216**.21, 24, 25, 32

    to Communications Data Bill **245**.8

    to environmental issues **218**.14

    to film classification **196**.15-16

    to food from cloned animals **211**.6, 11, 12, 14

    to genetically modified food **208**.18, 29-30; **211**.5

    on health care and the NHS **251**.19-22

    to human rights **229**.11-12

    to immigration **220**.22-3, 26, 27-8

    to inter-faith relations **212**.30-31

    to LGBT people **225**.11-13

    to mental ill health **201**.23

    to population growth **220**.10

    to press self-regulation **196**.6

    to same-sex marriage **244**.22, 24-5, 27, 28, 29

    to social mobility and earnings **219**.15

    terrorism fears following London bombings **212**.4

    to use of torture **229**.12, 22

public grief **192**.7-8

    memorial websites **192**.38-9

Public Health England **251**.25, 31

public interest and media regulation **210**.28

Public Order Act and film classification **196**.14

public sector cuts **227**.16

public sector fraud **207**.21, 22

public services

    open data policies **245**.12-13

    and population growth **220**.7

public transport

    and bicycles **200**.21

    city strategies **200**.30-31

    and disabled people **197**.11-12, 23

    effects of London bombings **212**.4

    high prices **200**.16

    as terrorism targets **212**.7

    usage **200**.3

    see also buses; railways

puerperal psychosis **190**.15

punishment *see* penalties; sentencing

Punishment of Incest Act 1908 **248**.35

pupil premium **209**.18, 24

pupils

    assaults on staff **209**.16

    attitudes to learning styles **209**.1-3

attitudes to school **209**.11
behaviour and teacher stress **209**.15
Puppet on a String report (Barnardo's) **246**.35-6
Purdy, Debbie **217**.24
Putting Patients First **251**.4

qualifications
academic and vocational **209**.1-3
see also A-levels; degrees; educational
achievement; GCSEs
Queen Elizabeth II **240**.22-3
quitting smoking *see* smoking, giving up
Quorn **214**.9
and vegan diet **214**.29

Race Online 2012 **230**.21
Race Relations Act **236**.1-3, 16, 21
'race to the bottom', banana industry **226**.35
racial discrimination **236**.1-39
definitions **236**.1-3
and drug laws **228**.34
against Gypsies and Travellers **236**.21-2
see also racism
racial equality, global public attitudes **229**.12
racial harassment **236**.2-3
racism **236**.3-16, 21-39
admission of racist feelings **236**.33
casual racism **236**.29-30
against East Europeans **236**.32
experiences of **236**.6-12, 25
in football **236**.9, 12, 13, 15, 25, 38
indirect racism **236**.28
and mental problems in young people **201**.2
against Muslims *see* Islamophobia
perceptions of **236**.3-5
in the police **236**.26-7
in schools **236**.15, 16
on Twitter **232**.38; **236**.31
violence **236**.13-15
see also discrimination; employment and racism;
ethnic
minorities; racial discrimination
racist bullying **232**.10, 11, 17; **236**.16
radiation exposure due to smoking **188**.9
radiative forcing (climate forcing) **216**.1
radicalism at universities **212**.13-14
radio
broadcasting regulations **210**.27
digital **210**.15
and sexually explicit song lyrics **238**.20
UK services **210**.3
RAF, and Strategic Defence and Security Review
213.19
railways

and disabled people **197**.11
high-speed rail **200**.35, 36, 37-9
light rail **200**.30, 33-4
prices **200**.16
usage statistics **200**.3
rainforests *see* forests
rape
definition **237**.12
myths about **237**.14
reporting **237**.13-14
and sexual imagery **238**.12
rapid-cycling bipolar disorder **201**.15
Rastafarianism and vegetarianism **214**.6
Real IRA (RIRA) **212**.14
reality TV **210**.9
and body image **234**.7
reasonable adjustments for disabled people
education providers **197**.23
service providers **197**.21
workplace **197**.24
recession
and abortion rate **231**.13
and employment **183**.1-2
and gender pay gap **221**.23
impact on immigration **220**.31
and lone parent families **191**.13
and students' plans **209**.31
reclassification of cannabis **186**.4-5, 32-3
public opinion **186**.31
recombinant DNA technologies *see* genetic
modification
recovery programmes for offenders **223**.23-4
recruitment age, Armed Services **213**.15-16
recruitment of employees
and age discrimination **239**.12-13
Disability Symbol **197**.26-7
effects of recession **183**.1
and race discrimination **236**.20
use of social media **227**.38
recycling **218**.11; **242**.22-4, 33
and China's ban on plastic waste **242**.19
fines **242**.30
government policies **242**.3, 4
incentives **242**.31
increase in **242**.6
organic waste *see* composting waste
statistics **218**.12
red hair as cause of bullying **232**.16
red squirrels, Scotland **193**.37
reduce, reuse, recycle **218**.11
reducing waste **218**.11
see also recycling
redundancy
and disability discrimination **197**.24-5
emotional impact **183**.10-11
effect of recession **183**.2
referendum on Scottish independence **240**.32
refugees **235**.27
due to climate change **216**.10-11
see also asylum seekers
refuges **220**.36-7
environmental **220**.39
for male victims of domestic abuse **224**.11

for teenage victims of relationship abuse **224**.19
refusal to engage (indirect racism) **236**.28
regeneration effect of tourism **222**.4
regenerative medicine
    attitudes to **211**.6
    see also embryonic stem cell research; stem cell
research
registering a death **192**.29-30
regional and local government **240**.21, 27
regional nationalism **240**.8
regulation
    animal experiments **233**.28, 33
    assisted suicide **217**.8
    broadcasters **196**.18-21
    films **196**.13-16
    food additives **205**.15
    food labelling **205**.11-12
    health care **251**.25-6, 31-2
    herbal medicine **195**.4, 33, 34-5, 37-8
    Internet **196**.31, 36-7; **246**.7-8, 15-16
    media **210**.27-9, 34
    obscene publications 22-3
    press **196**.6
    private landlords **253**.12-13
    see also legislation
Regulation of Investigative Powers Act (RIPA)
245.32
Rehabilitation of Offenders Act **223**.27
relationships
    effect of child abuse **248**.4
    effect of pornography **246**.1, 11
    ending
        civil partnerships **244**.30-31
        see also divorce; separation
    and money worries **250**.33
    problems and suicide **199**.24
    and stress **206**.18
    trends **191**.3-4
    see also marriage
relative poverty **235**.2-3
relaxation
    and anxiety **206**.12
    and mental health **252**.25-6
    and stress **206**.34, 35
Release campaign for decriminalisation of drugs
possession **228**.34
religion **215**.1-39
    and abortion **231**.19, 39
    attitudes to **212**.30-31l **215**.7-8
    in Britain **215**.5-6, 8, 14, 15-16
    and the Census **215**.5
    and discrimination **215**.23-5; **225**.34, 35
    effects of **215**.7-8
    and euthanasia **217**.2, 4, 6
    faith schools *see* faith schools
    funeral traditions **192**.34-6
    and the law **215**.26-7
    media coverage **215**.13
    as natural human inclination **215**.16
    and pornography **246**.1
    religious observance in Britain **215**.5-6 ,8, 14, 15-
      16
    religious belief and same-sex marriage **244**.19,

23, 25, 29
    statistics **215**.5-6
    surveys **215**.5-6, 7-8, 15-16
    in USA **215**.6
    and vegetarianism **214**. 5, 6, 13
    see also churches; individual religions
religious discrimination at work **215**.23-4
religious education and faith schools **209**.23
religious freedom, global public attitudes **229**.12
religious marriage ceremonies **244**.2, 4, 8, 9
    civil partnerships **244**.17
    same-sex couples **244**.19
religious offence **196**.11-12
religious organizations hosting civil partnerships
    225.32
religious slaughter **233**.16
religious tolerance **215**.23-39
    and Islam **212**.32
religiously motivated crime
    anti-Muslim hate crime **215**.28-30
remarriage **244**.3
remembrance of the deceased **192**.10
    memorial websites **192**.38-9
    see also funerals
remittances from migrants **220**.21, 35
remote gambling *see* online gambling
remote working **227**.2-3
rendition of Libyan terror suspects **229**.22
renewable energy **204**.1, 2-8, 11-22, 25-7, 32;
    218.10
    biofuels **204**.3, 26, 32, 34, 39
    hydro power **204**.19, 27
    microgeneration **204**.35-6
    policies
        EU **204**.30-31
        UK **204**.7-8, 28-9
    subsidies **204**.4
    wave energy **204**.20, 26
    see also energy efficiency; solar energy; wind
energy
rented accommodation **253**.1, 10
    disability rights **197**.21-2
    need for regulation **253**.11, **253**.12-13
reoffending rates
    children **223**.31
    and employment **223**.26
reparative therapy, homosexuality **225**.2
repeat abortions **231**.11-12
reporters, female **210**.7
reproductive cloning **211**.22, 24-7
    see also human reproductive cloning
reproductive ethics **247**.22-39
reproductive immunology **247**.8
research cloning **211**.32
resin, cannabis (hashish) **186**.2, 7, 9
resource consumption **218**.7-8, 13-14
    and population growth **220**.11-12, 14, 15
    water **218**.33
Respect Yourself website **237**.37
respiratory health
    and cannabis **186**.15, 28
    lung cancer **186**.15; **188**.6, 8
    and passive smoking **188**.5, 10-11

and smoking **188**.5
responsible travel **222**.35
  definition **222**.25
  see also ecotourism
restorative justice **223**.28-9
retail industry
  crowdsourcing of CCTV monitoring **245**.30
  and environmentalism **207**.34
  and gender stereotyping **238**.34
  independent sector **207**.28
  and *Let Girls Be Girls* campaign **238**.9
  and sexualized products for children **238**.2-3, 5-6, 9, 31
  and shopper surveillance **245**.34-5
  statistics **207**.1
retargeting **230**.5
retirement **239**.14
  forced retirement **183**.14-15
  saving for **250**.33, 36
  working after retirement age **239**.16, 18
  see also pensions
reusing goods **218**.11
Reuters, social media guidelines **210**.32
Reverse Seasonal Affective Disorder **190**.7
rhinoceros, declining numbers **193**.1-2
rice, GM **208**.19, 29, 35
rich-poor gap
  global **226**.17-18
  UK **235**.12, 13
right to die *see* assisted suicide; euthanasia
rights
  in abortion **231**.17, 18
  children's *see* children's rights
  consumer *see* consumer rights
  to family life **245**.1
  and the Internet **230**.30, 37, 38-9
  to privacy **196**.38; **245**.1
  sexual **196**.36, 38
  see also human rights
Rights of the Child, UN Convention on the **202**.2; **229**.24-6, 29
riots of 2011
  and CCTV **245**.29
  children's sentences **223**.29
  reasons for **223**.8
  young people's reactions **223**.9-11
RIPA (Regulation of Investigative Powers Act) **245**.32
RIRA (Real IRA) **212**.14
risk behaviour
  international trends **252**.9-10
  and staying out late without parents knowing **252**.11-12
  see also alcohol abuse; drug abuse
Ritalin **252**.33, 34
road accidents **200**.12
  see also drink-driving
road charging **200**.9, 10
  congestion charging **200**.17-18
  public attitudes **200**.6
road tax (Vehicle Excise Duty) **200**.7
road traffic
  pollution *see* pollution and transport

  see also cars
roads
  arguments against building new roads **200**.7-8
  economic effects of new roads **200**.8
  funding **200**.6, 7, 9-10
  patterns of use **200**.5
  road surface material made from plastic bags **242**.28
  shared by cars and bikes **200**.18
  see also road charging
Robin Hood tax **235**.13-15
roll-your-own cigarettes **188**.19
Roman Catholics *see* Catholic Church
romance and marriage **244**.4
Romanian migrants as victims of rasism **236**.32
rough sleeping **189**.4, 16-17
  government targets **189**.8
  and mental health **189**.11
  young people **189**.23
  see also homelessness
Rowntree, Seebohm **219**.11
Royal Air Force and Strategic Defence and Security Review **213**.19
Royal Family **240**.23
Royal Navy and Strategic Defence and Security Review **213**.18-19
RSPCA (Royal Society for the Prevention of Cruelty to Animals) **233**.1
rubbish *see* waste
rumination syndrome **249**.8
runaways **189**.24, 25
running **241**.31, 32
  ability to run 100m **241**.13
  Zombies, Run! fitness app **241**.38-9
Russia, privacy rights **245**.4

S

SAD (Seasonal Affective Disorder) **190**.2, 6-7, 22
safe houses *see* refuges
Safe Routes to Schools (SRS) projects **200**.2
safe sex **237**.1-2
  see also contraception
Safer Sex in the Adult Film Industry Act **246**.5
safety
  children **248**.9-11
  complementary and alternative medicine **195**.2, 12-13, 34, 37-8
  and cycling **200**.21
  and food additives **205**.15
  food from cloned animals **211**.18, 19
  of genetically modified food **208**.1, 2, 24
  human cloning **211**.26, 27
  and the Human Rights Act **229**.3
  and self-harm **199**.6, 7-8
  at work, young people **183**.28
safety and the Internet **232**.26-7; **230**.22-9
  children's safety **238**.5, 15, 26; **248**.10-11, 12
  identity fraud **230**.24, 30
  network filters **238**.16, 25, 26
  parental controls **238**.5

Safetynet petition **238**.26
social networking **230**.23-4
see also cyberbullying
salaries
graduates **183**.36; **185**.32-4
see also earnings; wages
salmon, genetically modified **208**.31, 39
Salmon Report on the NHS **251**.2
salt intake **205**.5
health effects **205**.25-6
need to reduce salt content of food **205**.18
Samaritans **199**.20, 22, 31, 35
same-sex relationships
adoption **225**.34
civil partnerships **244**.16-18
in religious buildings **225**.32; **244**.17
and domestic abuse **224**.5, 12-13
human rights **229**.31-2
and IVF treatment **247**.27
marriage **225**.33; **244**.19-29
medieval Europe **244**.5
and surrogacy **247**.18-19
sanitation in developing countries **218**.31-3, 36
Sarah's Law **248**.35
SARC (sexual assault referral centre) **237**.14
SAT aptitude tests **219**.32
Sativex **228**.26
saturated fats **205**.1, 3, 24
Saudi Arabia, death penalty **229**.37
savings
children **250**.39
lack of **250**.4, 26
for old age **239**.14; **250**.33, 36
young people **250**.26, 27-8
saviour siblings **211**.32; **247**.37-8
Say Yes to 21st Century Sex and Relationships Education campaign **237**.36
schizo affective disorder **190**.9
schizophrenia **185**.8; **201**.16-17
and cannabis use **186**.10, 12, 31, 32; **228**.8
scholarships, students **250**.24
school bullying **232**.1, 5-6, 17
dealing with bullying **232**.4, 18
racist bullying **232**.10, 11, 17
staff experiencing cyberbullying **232**.33, 34-6
school leaving age and teenage pregnancies **182**.31
school meals **252**.30-31
and children's health **241**.20, 21
World Food Programme **229**.28
school nurses **252**.15
School Standard and Framework Act 1998 **225**.7
schools **209**.1-26
academies **209**.25, 26
admission systems **219**.24
assaults on staff **209**.16
attendance during pregnancy **182**.6
and body image **234**.11, 21, 29-30
bullying *see* school bullying
carbon footprint reduction **200**.19-20
and CCTV **245**.36-7
and childhood obesity **241**.20
and children in poverty **235**.22

children's attitudes to **209**.1-3, 11
citizenship education **240**.1-2, 38
collecting data on children **245**.16
curriculum reform **209**.5
developing countries **229**.27-8
and disabled children **197**.5, 23
children with learning problems **197**.14-15
and ending violence against women and girls **224**.29
employers' involvement **219**.26
ex-service personnel as mentors **213**.32
faith-based **209**.22-3, 24; **215**.17-22
and financial education **250**.17, 19
free schools **209**.19-21
faith-based **215**.21-2
and genderstereotype awareness **238**.14
girl's non-attendance **221**.38-9
and healthy eating **205**.6-7
HPV (cervical cancer) vaccination **237**.31
ICT education **230**.13
journeys to **200**.1-2, 19-20
knife crime education **223**.16-17
and LGBT people **225**.5-8
online privacy education **245**.26
parent satisfaction **209**.21
parental presuure **209**.4
performance data publication **245**.12
and physical activity **241**.9
PSHE education, sexualisation and gender stereotyping **238**.4, 11, 14
and racism **236**.15, 16
same-sex marriage education **244**.21, 24
school system reform **209**.6
school type and pupil's degree perfomance **219**.32
selective, and social mobility **219**.31
self-harm support **199**.5-6
sex education *see* sex education
and sexual health services **182**.31
single-sex **221**.30-32
and social mobility **219**.18, 23, 28, 31
and special educational needs **197**.14-15, 23
sports, Olympic-style competition **198**.5
standards **209**.7-10
support for children with suicidal feelings **199**.31, 33
travel plans **200**.2
and violent extremism **212**.12
vocational courses **183**.31
Youth Parliament manifesto **240**.38
see also education; National Curriculum; secondary schools; teachers
SCNT *see* somatic-cell nuclear transfer
Scotland
abortion law **231**.3
crime statistics **223**.2
drug strategy **228**.24
empty homes **253**.33
euthanasia legislation rejection **217**. 30
feelings of Scottish identity **240**.8, 12, 18
gangs and knife crime **223**.6-7
Gypsy Travellers **236**.22
health and physical activity **241**.1-4

homelessness **189**.3

homophobic crime **225**.30

independence **240**.5, 6, 32

life on the streets **189**.18-20

Olympic Games legacy **241**.10

palliative care **217**.18

parliament **240**.27

physical activity levels **241**.1

red squirrels **193**.37

reintroduction of animals **193**.33-4

suicides **199**.26

teenage abortions **182**.2

teenage pregnancy **182**.2, 7

sea level rise **216**.9, 16-17, 20-21

effect on island nations **220**.38

seal hunting **233**.22-3

seas *see* marine environments

Seasonal Affective Disorder (SAD) **190**.2, 6-7, 22

SeaWorld, slavery case **233**.21

second-hand smoke *see* passive smoking

secondary infertility **247**.4

secondary schools

see A-levels; GCSEs; schools

secondment **183**.18

secret self and self-harm **199**.11

Secretary of State for Health **251**.30

secularism

as argument for banning burqa **215**.36

in Britain **215**.15

security

as reason for banning burqa **215**.35

and social networking **210**.30-31

seed hybridization **211**.2

selective eating **249**.23-4

selective schools and social mobility **219**.31

Selective Serotonin Re-uptake Inhibitors (SSRIs)
190.10, 32-3

and suicide **190**.24

selenium

in red meat **214**.34-5

and vegetarian diets **214**.29

self-affirmation **199**.6; **234**.3

Self Assessment tax returns **250**.13

self-blame *see* blame, feelings of

self-defence and protection against bullying **232**.21

self-directed violence *see* self-harm; suicide

self-employment

graduates **185**.30

and National Insurance **250**.15

self-esteem

Dove campaign **234**.33

and child abuse **248**.4

and eating disorders **249**.3

impact of pornography **246**.1

see also body image

self-harm **190**.28-9; **199**.1-19; **252**.22-3

avoidance techniques **199**.5-6, 7, 8

and bullying **232**.9

case studies **199**.9

and depression **190**.23

definition **199**.1, 4, 20

effects **199**.11

following child abuse **248**.5

minimizing damage **199**.7

prevalence **199**.4

reasons **199**.2, 5, 10-12

risk factors **199**.4

risk groups **199**.1-2, 4-5

sources of help **199**.2-3, 5

self-help **199**.2, 5-6, 7, 8

and suicide **199**.12, 23-4

treatment **199**.13-14, 15

self help

anxiety problems **206**.12

for depression **252**.19

for eating disorders **249**.3-4

improving mental health **252**.25-6

for stress **206**.3-4, 27

self-image *see* body image

self-loathing as cause of self-harm **199**.10

self management training and bipolar disorder
190.11

self-poisoning, emergency treatment **199**.14

self-regulation of the press **196**.6

self-stigma

HIV sufferers **243**.17

mental illness **201**.28

Send My Sister to School campaign **221**.35

sentencing **223**.19-20, 21

children **223**.29, 30

community sentences **223**.20, 23

for drugs offences **228**.23, 28-31

Legal Aid, Sentencing and Punishment of
Offenders Bill **223**.25

and maturity of young offenders **223**.33-4

terrorism offences **212**.9-10, 19

separation

couples unable to afford to separate **244**.38-9

effect on children **191**.1, 9; **244**.36-7

online help **244**.34

see also divorce

serotonin and mental health **201**.33

sex

attitudes to, effect of pornography **246**.1, 2-3

and cannabis use **186**.29

sex discrimination

in the Army **213**.13-14

see also gender inequality

sex education **182**.28-9, 32-5; **238**.4, 14-15; **237**.15-
16, 33-9

failure of **237**.33, 35-6

and LBGT relationships **225**.7

role of parents **182**.34-5

in schools **237**.15-16, 35-6

and unplanned pregnancies **237**.8

website **237**.37

sex offences, statistics **223**.5

sex offenders

and IVF treatment **247**.27

registration, and Human Rights Act **229**.6

Sex Offenders Act 1997 **248**.35

sex-selection

abortion **231**.18, 30-31

of embryos **247**.35, 36

sex stereotyping *see* gender stereotyping

sex tourism **202**.18-19

sex trafficking **229**.17; **246**.23, 25, 30-32
    of boys and men **246**.39
    of children **246**.35-6, 37
    definition **246**.30
    and prostitution **229**.19-20; **246**.29, 33
sex workers
    advice for **246**.21-3
    and HIV **243**.6
    see also prostitution
sexting **221**.9-10; **230**.26-7; **238**.23-4; **246**.11
sexual abuse **248**.3, 5-7, 26-31
    among children **238**.17; **248**.13
    and children's mental health problems **201**.3
    definition **248**.5, 26
    as domestic abuse **224**.1, 3
    effects **248**.26
    getting help **248**.26-7
    perpetrators **248**.6, 26
    prevalence **248**.5-6
    support for victims in court **248**.39
    among young people **238**.15
sexual abusers *see* sex offenders
sexual assault
    definition **237**.12
    reporting **237**.13-14
    see also rape
sexual assault referral centre (SARC) **237**.14
sexual behaviour
    and alcohol **194**.19, 23
    teenagers **182**.1; **237**.15-17
sexual bullying **221**.11
sexual consent and the law **237**.12-14
sexual content on the Internet **196**.36-9
    child abuse **196**.39
sexual exploitation of children **202**.16-31
    case study **202**.24-6
    effects of **202**.22-3
    perpetrators **202**.20-21
    and sex tourism **202**.18-19
    see also child pornography; child prostitution
sexual health **237**.1-17
    and cannabis use **186**.29
    safe sex **237**.1-2
    see also contraception; sex education; sexually
transmitted infections
sexual health services in schools **182**.31
sexual offences, statistics **223**.5
Sexual Offences Act **246**.17, 18; **248**.1, 35
sexual orientation **225**.1-18
    altering **225**.2, 16, 17-18
    attitudes to **225**.11-13
    and bullying *see* homophobic bullying
    causes **225**.1-2, 15-16
    definitions **225**.3, 5, 19-20
    discovering **225**.1
    discrimination **225**.9-10, 28-9, 35
    and the law **225**.28-39
    and US military **225**.38-9
    see also gay men; lesbians; LGBT people;
transgender people
Sexual Orientation Change Efforts (SOCE) **225**.17-18
sexual rights **196**.36

threats to **196**.38
sexual transmission of HIV **243**.1
sexualisation **238**.1-39; **246**.12, 13
    Bailey Review **238**.2, 5-7, 8, 33, 34
    of children **238**.1-37, 38-9
    children's clothing and products **238**.1, 5-6, 8-9,
      10, 13, 31, 32-3, 36
    definition **238**.1
    effect of the media **196**.25-6; 3, 13, 32-3
    effects on children **238**.2, 8, 9
    of women **221**.34; **238**.37-8
    of boys **238**.1, 3
    of young girls **221**.9-10; **238**.1, 3, 8-9, 13, 27-33
      parents' complicity **238**.36-7
sexuality *see* sexual orientation
sexually transmitted infections (STIs) **237**.1-2, 18-25
    chlamydia **237**.20, 22, 24; **252**.2, 3
    and fertility **247**.5
    genital warts **237**.20
    gonorrhoea **237**.20-21, 24-5
    hepatitis B **237**.21
    herpes **237**.20
    infection rates **237**.10, 24-5
    knowledge about **237**.23
    protection against **237**.1-2, 4, 18-19
    pubic lice (crabs) **237**.21
    symptoms **237**.4, 19, 20-21, 22
    syphilis **237**.21
    testing for **237**.22, 24
      gay and bisexual men **243**.9
    and young people **237**.24-5; **252**.2, 3
    see also AIDS; HIV
shared ownership home-buying schemes **253**.8
Sharia law **215**.11-12
Shelter **189**.25, 30, 34
shoes, leather, and vegetarianism **214**.13
shopping
    addiction to **207**.6
    Internet *see* Internet shopping
    shopper surveillance **245**.34-5
    see also consumer rights; consumerism;
consumers; retail industry
shops, empty **207**.9
Shulman, Alexandra **234**.5-6
siblings, saviour **211**.32; **247**.37-8
sickness absence **183**.8, 9
    due to smoking **188**.22
    going to work when sick **183**.9
sight problems with ageing **239**.4, 25-6
Sikhism **215**.3
    and abortion **231**.19
    funerals **192**.35
    and pornography **246**.1
    and vegetarianism **214**.6
single parents *see* lone parents
single-sex education
    boys **221**.30
    girls **221**.31-2
Single Transferable Vote **240**.29
SIV (self-inflicted violence) *see* self-harm
skunk (cannabis) **186**.9, 11
    mental health effects **186**.13
sleep

and mental health, teenagers **201**.7
young people **252**.4, 27, 28
sleep-related eating disorder **249**.8
sleeping rough *see* rough sleeping
slums **235**.36-8
slum tourism **222**.16, 33-4
slutwalk protests **221**.12
small businesses
costs of fraud **207**.22
difficulties **227**.8
start-ups **227**.5
statistics **227**.6
smart drugs **252**.33, 34
smartphones **210**.11, 13-14
booking travel **222**.9
children viewing inappropriate content **238**.19
and shopper surveillance **245**.34
Smedley, Peter (assisted suicide) **217**.20
smokeless tobacco **188**.11
smoking **188**.1-38
age of starting smoking **188**.3
and cancer **188**.8-11
cannabis *see* cannabis
children **252**.37-9
costs of **188**.15, 22-3
effects on appearance **188**.14
effects on fertility **247**.3, 5
giving up **188**.6, 13-14, 17
benefits **188**.6, 9
pregnant women **188**.30-32
reasons for giving up **188**.13
tips on giving up **188**.13-14, 16
and health **188**.5-12, 15, 18, 19, 22
benefits of giving up **188**.6, 9
passive smoking **188**.5, 10-11, 12
in pregnancy **188**.11, 31
imagery influencing young people **188**.24-6
and life expectancy **188**.18
men **188**.1, 3
effects of smoking 15
passive smoking **188**.5, 10-11, 12
and pregnancy **182**.15; **188**.11, 30-32
prevalence **188**.1-3
pro-smoking views **188**.34-5
and stress **206**.33
students **185**.9
women **188**.1, 3
effects of smoking **188**.15
pregnant women **182**.15; **188**.11, 30-32
young people **252**.1-2, 31, 35, 37-8
influences on smoking habits **188**.24-8
stopping smoking **188**.13-14
smoothies, and fluid intake **205**.28
smuggling, tobacco **188**.23
snuff **188**.11
social activity, older people **239**.27, 38, 39
social care *see* care services for older people
social capital and health **219**.12
social class
and health **219**.11-13
middle classes **219**.1-2, 9-10
working classes **219**.3-4, 5-6
and alcohol consumption, teenagers **194**.24

and educational attainment **219**.29-30
see also social mobility
social drinking **194**.17
social exclusion **235**.2
and sexual orientation **225**.9-10
social factors
and gambling **203**.32-3
and suicide **199**.24
social gambling **203**.12
social housing **253**.13-14
lifetime tenancies **253**.15
and immigrants **220**.28, 29
social isolation *see* loneliness
social marketing and sex education **182**.39
social media *see* social networking
social mobility **219**.14-39
and education **219**.18, 22, 23, 25-6, 27-8, 34-5
government strategy **219**.17-21
and higher education **185**.18
perceptions of **219**.15
prejudice against **219**.4
and the professions **185**.38-9
rate of **219**.14
Social Mobility and Child Poverty Commission
219.19
social model of disability **197**.2
social networking **210**.5, 12, 14; **252**.9
birth parents contacting adopted children **247**.16
and bullying **232**.25, 26-7, 28
and business ethics **227**.37-9
and data mining **245**.23-4
eating disorder promotion **249**.29, 30
and gambling **203**.17
and gender **230**.2, 3
parents monitoring children's use **245**.26-7
and privacy **210**.33-4; **230**.33-4; 18, 25-6
and racism **236**.31
and relationship abuse **224**.16-17
reporting inappropriate content **232**.35
Reuters guidelines **210**.32
safety **230**.23-4
security issues **210**.30-31
and travel **222**.9
see also Facebook
social security benefits *see* state benefits
social welfare
history **219**.11
see also state benefits
social welfare law problems and mental health,
young people **201**.29-30
socio-economic groups
and academic performance **209**.13-14
and higher education participation **209**.34-5
and life expectancy **188**.18
and smoking **188**.2, 3, 33
see also social class
sofa surfing **189**.7
soft drinks **205**.5, 28
Soil Association **205**.33
solar energy
solar electricity **204**.3, 25, 35–6
from space **204**.39
subsidies **204**.7

water heating **204**.3, 21-2, 25, 35
soldiers, child *see* child soldiers
soliciting **246**.23
solvent and volatile substance abuse **228**.7, 15
somatic-cell nuclear transfer (SCNT) **211**.24
   see also therapeutic cloning
SOPA (Stop Online Piracy Act) **230**.35-6, 37
Sorting Out Separation web app **244**.34
South Africa
   as gap year destination **222**.19
   privacy rights **245**.4
   wellbeing of older people **239**.9
sovereign debt **226**.5
spa holidays 5
space, solar energy collection **204**.39
space rationing (housing policy) **253**.17
space tourism **222**.17-18
SPCA (Society for the Prevention to Cruelty to Animals) **233**.1
Special Educational Needs (SEN) **197**.14-15, 23
species conservation, zoos **233**.25, 26
species loss **193**.13; **220**.6
   England **193**.31-2
   Galapagos Islands **193**.24-5
species reintroduction, Britain **193**.33-4
speech pathologists **197**.4
spending
   and budgeting **250**.37-8
   on communications **210**.12
   on holidays **222**.5, 6-7
   household **207**.7, 8
   personal **207**.6
sperm production and fertility **247**.2, 3
spiking drinks **194**.8-10
spina bifida **197**.3
spiritual brotherhoods **244**.5
sponsorship and advertising to children **207**.39
sport **198**.1-39
   betting **203**.8
   and bullying **232**.1-2, 7
   for children **241**.35-6
   and drugs *see* drugs in sport
   and ethnic minorities **236**.12
   legacy of Olympic Games **241**.9, 10
   and racism **236**.9, 12, 13, 15, 25, 38, 39
   and inclusion **198**.18-26
   poverty gap **241**.29-30
   sexualized promotion of sportswomen **238**.37-8
   sports events and sex trafficking **229**.20
   trends **198**.1-17
   see also football; Olympic Games
Sport England, funding for disability sport **198**.18
spread betting **203**.4
Spurs football club, 'anti-Semitic' chants **236**.39
squirrels
   grey **193**.38
   red, Scotland **193**.37
St John's wort **252**.19
Staff Survey, NHS **251**.18
stalking **224**.5
starchy foods **205**.2-3
start-ups, business **227**.5
state benefits
   benefit fraud **219**.5-6
   after bereavement **192**.30-31, 32
   disabled people **197**.31-4
     benefit cuts **229**.32
   maternity pay **191**.38
   and National Insurance **250**.15-16
   rented housing discrimination against claimants **253**.12
   and welfare reform bill **235**.9
   see also disability benefits
statements of special education needs **197**.23
status dogs **233**.4
statutory homelessness **189**.3-4
Statutory Maternity Pay **191**.38
staycations **222**.5
staying out late without parents knowing **252**.11-12
stem cell lines **211**.30
stem cell research **211**.29-37
   embryonic **211**.29-32
   ethical issues **211**.30-31, 34
   induced pluripotent stem cells **211**.35-7
stem cell therapy **211**.30
   for multiple sclerosis **211**.38-9
stem cell transplants, saviour siblings **211**.32; **247**.37-8
stem cells **211**.28, 29-30
   embryonic **211**.28, 29-30, 35-6
   from aborted fetuses **211**.33
   iPS **211**.35-7
   tissue-specific (adult) **211**.28, 29
stepfamilies **191**.10
stereotyping
   age **239**.4-5, 6
   gender *see* gender stereotyping
   racial **236**.34
sterilization **182**.19
steroids *see* anabolic agents/steroids
STIs *see* sexually transmitted infections
stigma about living with HIV **243**.15-17
stimulants (uppers) **228**.3
   signs of use **228**.14
   and sports drug abuse **198**.29
   see also ecstasy
stomach cancer, effect of salt intake **205**.26
stop and search
   anti-Muslim discrimination **212**.28-9
   Terrorism Act **212**.16
Stop Online Piracy Act (SOPA) **230**.35-6, 37
stopping smoking *see* smoking, giving up
straddling bus **200**.29
stranger danger **248**.9-10
Strategic Defence and Security Review **213**.17-19
   criticism of **213**.20-21
street design for sustainable transport **200**.30
street homelessness **189**.18-20
   young people **189**.27-8
Street View (Google) and privacy **210**.33; **245**.38-9
stress
   causes **206**.17-31
   complications **206**.4
   coping with **206**.32-9
   definition **206**.24
   and exams **252**.16-17
   self help **206**.3-4, 27

signs and symptoms **206**.1-2, 7-9, 17, 19
statistics on **206**.5, 21
stay-at-home parents **191**.35
students **206**.38-9
treatment **206**.2-4
work-related *see* work-related stress
young people **252**.4, 5-6
strip clubs **246**.23
strokes **239**.26; **241**.3-4
effect of salt intake **205**.25
stem cell therapy **211**.33
students
accommodation **185**.7; **209**.30
binge drinking **252**.36
black students, employment prospects **236**.19-20
dropping out **209**.32
eating disorders **249**.15
housing **185**.7
lifestyle **209**.30-33
mental health **185**.8
and money matters **209**.31-2
budgeting **185**.3, 11
costs of a university education **185**.11, 17, 36
financial help **206**.39
graduate starting salaries **185**.33-4
grants and loans **185**.2; **250**.22-5
satisfaction with course **185**.4-5
and stress **206**.38-9
student life **185**.3-4
Students Union **209**.30
study leave **183**.18
submissive victims of bullying **232**.8
subsidies
definition **226**.30
impact on developing countries **226**.33
substance abuse
and depression **190**.3
and homelessness **189**.10-11
see also alcohol; drug abuse; solvent abuse
suction aspiration (abortion) **231**.7
sugar
in diet **205**.3
labelling rules **205**.12
and mental health **252**.25
suicidal feelings **199**.23
and bullying **232**.9
getting help **199**.20, 22, 28
how to help someone **199**.22, 25-6, 30, 32-3
reasons **199**.20, 24, 30
young people **190**.29
suicide **199**.20-39
and anti-depressants **190**.24
and bullying **232**.9
copycat suicides **199**.36
and depression **190**.21, 23
and the Internet **199**.33, 35
and the media **199**.35, 36
myths **199**.27
reasons for **199**.24, 30
risk factors for **199**.20-21, 31-2
risk groups **199**.20-21, 24-5
and self-harm **199**.12, 23-4

statistics **190**.27; **199**.21; **252**.1
suicide terrorism
condemned by Islam **215**.10-11
Great Britain **212**.5-6
use of children **212**.11-12
support for suicidal people **199**.20, 22, 26, 30
children **199**.33
men **199**.38
Samaritans **199**.20, 22, 31, 35
warning signs **190**.26-7; **199**.22, 25, 29-30, 31-2
young people **190**.26, 27; **199**.21, 31-3; **252**.1
see also assisted suicide; physician-assisted suicide (PAS)
Suicide Act and assisted suicide **217**.24
summer depression **190**.7
super-farms **233**.3, 9-11
super-fast broadband **210**.15
supermarkets
and banana prices **226**.35
and meat free products **214**.7
threat to local shops **207**.26, 27
vegetarian food availability **214**.9
Supplementary Vote (SV) **240**.29
support groups
gamblers **203**.25,
stress and anxiety sufferers **206**.3, 12; **252**.14-15
surgical abortion **231**.7
surrogacy **247**.18-19
health risks, surrogate mothers in India **247**.20-21
surveillance **245**.28-39
CCTV **245**.28-32, 36-7
by the government **245**.32
by the retail sector **245**.34-5
in schools **245**.36-7
suspended prison sentences **223**.19
sustainability
cities **218**.6
eco-towns **253**.36
fisheries **218**.23
and marine environments **218**.22
and population growth **218**.5
and resource use **218**.7-8
sustainable agriculture **214**.14, 20-21
sustainable development **226**.3-4
sustainable housing **253**.37
Sustainable Restaurant Association **242**.39
sustainable tourism **222**.8-9, 21-3
definition **222**.25
see also ecotourism; responsible travel
sustainable transport networks **200**.30-31
swearing on television **196**.21
Sweden
free schools **209**.20
health care **251**.9
importing waste for waste-to-energy plants **242**.37
LGBT equality policy **225**.13
modeling agencies targeting eating disorder
sufferers **249**.26
sex education **237**.34
swimming, funding cuts **198**.6-7
Switzerland, assisted suicide **217**.2
syphilis **237**.21

T

Takhi (Przewalski's horse) **233**.26
TalkTalk, Internet filter service **238**.16, 25
talent identification
    Olympic sports **198**.8-10
    Paralympic sports **198**.22
talking
    about dying **192**.8, 24
    and the grieving process **192**.5
    see also communication
talking therapies **190**.5, 11, 34; **252**.19
Tanzania, education improvements **229**.27
tapenadol, classification **228**.25
tar, in cigarette smoke **188**.4
    effect on heart **188**.7
    effect on lungs **188**.5
tariffs **226**.13, 26-7
taxation
    air travel **222**.14-15
    after death **192**.32
    Council Tax **250**.14
    ending 50p rate **219**.7
    as ethical investment issue **227**.33
    on financial sector **235**.13-15
    high earners opinions of **227**.25
    Income Tax **250**.13
    and multination corporations **227**.32-3
    National Insurance **250**.15
    and NHS funding **251**.20-21
    and road building **200**.7
    tax havens **227**.34-6
    tobacco **188**.23
    and trade **226**.13, 26-7
    on unhealthy food **241**.20-21
    VAT **250**.14
taxis and disabled people **197**.12
tea, and fluid intake **205**.27
teachers
    assaults by pupils **209**.16
    attitudes to school learning styles **209**.1-3
    and cyberbullying **232**.33, 34-6
    faith schools **209**.23
    influence on children's attainment **219**.33
    not encouraging Oxbridge applications **185**.24
    racist bullying **236**.16
    and same-sex marriage education **244**.21, 24
    stress caused by pupil behaviour **209**.15
technology use
    business trends **227**.1-3
    Middle Britain **219**.2
    supporting care for older people **239**.38
teenage depression **190**.25-7, 30
teenage mothers **182**.16
    supervised homes **182**.17-18
teenage parents **182**.14-18
    see also teenage fathers; teenage mothers
teenage pregnancies **182**.1-13
    and abortion **182**.12-13
    options **182**.6, 8-9
    public perceptions of **182**.13
    risks **182**.11, 37
    statistics **182**.2, 7, 10-11, 37

    unplanned **237**.8, 10
Teenage Pregnancy Strategy **182**.24, 25-6, 27
teenage relationship abuse **224**.4, 16-21, 35-6
teenage suicide, warning signs **190**.26-7
teenagers *see* young people
teeth and human diet **214**.12
teetotallers **194**.11-12
telecommunications
    broadband services **210**.15; **230**.6-8
    international comparisons **210**.13-15
    prices, international comparisons **210**.14-15
    statistics **210**.10
    trends **210**.4-5, 10-16
telephones,   mobile *see* mobile phones
television
    and body image **234**.7, 19
    offensive language **196**.21, 24
    pre-watershed programming **238**.5
    reality television *see* reality television
    regulation **196**.18-20; **210**.27
    sexual content of programmes for young people
        238.13-14
    UK services **210**.3
    viewing habits **210**.4, 11
telomeres and ageing **239**.1
temperature of the earth
    changes **216**.8, 9
    measurement **216**.26-7
    see also climate change; global warming
temporary accommodation **189**.8
temporary class drug orders **228**.25
tenancy sustainment services **189**.34
tenants, protection **253**.11, 12-13
terminally ill people
    assisted suicide *see* assisted suicide
    and carer's grief **192**.6
    euthanasia *see* euthanasia
Territorial Army (TA) **213**.30
terrorism **212**.1-39
    and Communications Data Bill **245**.5
    counter-terrorism **212**.15-25
        legislation **212**.15-16, 19, 20
        police powers **212**.15-16
        review **212**.21-2, 26, 38-9
    definition **212**.1, 15
    effects **212**.2-3
    and Islam **212**.32
    Islamist **212**.8-10
    London bombings **212**.4, 5
    reasons for **212**.1
    suicide terrorism
      Great Britain **212**.5-6
      use of children **212**.11-12
    Terrorism Acts **212**.15-16, 19
    Terrorism Prevention and Investigation Measures
Bill **212**.20
    in the UK **212**.5-7, 8-10
        effect on the public **212**.4
        by Irish Republican groups **212**.14
        by Islamists **212**.8-10
Terry, John **236**.38
Tesco, virtual store **245**.35
test tube babies *see* in vitro fertilisation

tetrahydrocannabinol *see* THC
text message bullying **232**.17, 29
TfST (Time Off for Study or Training) **183**.29
Thailand as gap year destination **222**.19
THC (delta-9 tetrahydrocannabinol)
    and cannabis strength **186**.7, 22
    effects **186**.9
    in skunk **186**.13
therapeutic cloning **211**.9, 22-3
    research applications **211**.23
therapeutic use exemption, drugs in sport **198**.28
therapy, family *see* family therapy
thermohaline circulation **216**.8
Thinspo (Thinspiration) **249**.29, 30
Third World *see* developing countries
threats as domestic abuse **224**.1
three-parent IVF **247**.29-34
tidal power **204**.26
tigers
    as endangered species **193**.1, 18
    tiger tourism **222**.26
timber production, environmental impact **193**.4
time limit for abortion **231**.21-3
time management, and stress **206**.18, 34, 35
Time Off for Study or Training (TfST) **183**.29
tissue specific (adult) stem cells **211**.28, 29
TNCs *see* transnational corporations
tobacco
    advertising ban **188**.23
    chemical contents of smoke **188**.4, 9-10, 15
    and the economy **188**.22-3
    see also smoking
tobacco industry **188**.23
    tobacco pickers' health problems **188**.39
tobacco-specific nitrosamines (TSNAs) **188**.11
toll roads **200**.9, 10
Too Good to Waste campaign **242**.39
top jobs, gender gap **221**.13-22
torture
    public attitudes to **229**.12, 22
    UK complicity in **229**.21-3
    by US soldiers **212**.36-7
tourism
    alternative **222**.16, 24
    Britain as holiday destination **222**.2-3, 5, 11
    child sex tourism **202**.18-19
    and climate change **216**.12
    destination choice **222**.2-3, 11
    economic benefits **222**.4-5, 28, 30
    and endangered species **222**.26
    environmental impact **222**.21, 22, 25, 27, 28, 29
    and ethics **222**.31-2
    gap year destinations **222**.19
    holiday spending **222**.5, 6-7
    and London Olympics **222**.12-13
    slum tourism **222**.16, 33-4
    space tourism **222**.17-18
    sustainable tourism **222**.8-9, 21-3, 25
    trends **222**.1-3, 8-9
    volunteer tourism **222**.8, 27-8, 36-9
    see also ecotourism; holidays; responsible
tourism
toxic chemicals in tobacco smoke **188**.4, 9-10, 15

toxicity
    emissions from waste incineration **242**.35-6
    and GM crops **208**.27
    nanotechnology **208**.16
toys, colour coding and gender **221**.7-8
trade
    definition **226**.26
    international *see* international trade
trade in endangered species **193**.20-21
    ivory trade ban **193**.19
trade footprint **226**.34
trade in indecent articles **196**.23
trade justice **226**.29, 33
trade liberalisation *see* free trade
trade negotiations and WTO agreements **226**.8
trade rules **226**.27
    see also World Trade Organization
Traditional Herbal Medicines Registration Scheme
(THMRS) **195**.4, 35, 38
traditional medicine **195**.9, 10
    regulation difficulties **195**.36
    see also herbal medicines
traffic *see* road traffic
traffic pollution *see* pollution and transport
trafficking **229**.17-20
    children **202**.27-31
    definition **202**.1
    in UK **202**.27-9, 30, 31
    see also sex trafficking
training
    effect of recession **183**.2
    young people **183**.29
trains *see* railways
trams **200**.29, 33, 34
tranquilizers **194**.9
    and phobia treatment **206**.13
transgender people **225**.5, 19-27
    definitions **225**.19-20
    and domestic abuse **224**.5, 12-13
    experiences **225**.21-2
    hate crime against **225**.30-31
    and marriage **225**.27
transgenic technology *see* genetic modification
Transition to Adulthood (T2A) Alliance **223**.33
transnational corporations (TNCs) **226**.1, 27
transphobia **225**.7-8
transport **200**.1-39
    and disabled people **197**.11-12, 23
    electric vehicles **200**.26-9
    emissions *see* emissions
    and the environment **200**.14-39
    of food, environmental impact **205**.31
    and global poverty **200**.13
    and inequality **218**.3, 4
    noise **200**.14-15, 22
    policies **200**.15
    and schools **200**.1-2, 19-20
    sustainable transport networks **200**.30-31
    trends **200**.1-13
    see also air travel; cars; public transport; railways
transracial adoption **247**.16
transsexual people
    definition **225**.19

and marriage **225**.27; **244**.1
public figures **225**.25-6
transvestites **225**.19
trapping animals **193**.1
for fur **233**.18
trauma as cause of anxiety **206**.11
travel *see* air travel; transport; tourism
travel agents **222**.3
travel behaviour **222**.3
travel health advice **222**.10
travel information sources, new technologies **222**.9
Travellers and racial discrimination **236**.21-2
treatment
anxiety problems **206**.12; **252**.15
bipolar disorder **190**.10-11; **201**.15
dementia **239**.29
depression **190**.26, 31-9; **239**.31; **252**.19
drug abuse effects **228**.2
drug dependency **228**.16-18
eating disorders **249**.32-9
HIV **243**.3-4, 6, 32-5, 37-9
of homosexuality **225**.2, 16, 17-18
obesity **241**.18, 22
see also weight management
panic attacks **206**.16
phobias **206**.12-13
psychosis **201**.18-19
Seasonal Affective Disorder **190**.6-7
stress **206**.2-4
see also self help
Trekstock **240**.35
tricyclic antidepressants **190**.10-11, 33
Trojan gene effect **208**.39
trolling **232**.32, 37
tuberculosis and HIV sufferers
global incidence **243**.6, 27
UK incidence **243**.5
tuition fees, university **185**.11, 17, 29, 36
loans **250**.23
Turkey, domestic violence **224**.32-3
12 Step Programme **203**.25
Twitter **210**.18
criticism of Communications Data Bill **245**.6
and racist abuse **232**.38; **236**.31
two signature rule, abortions **231**.2

U

Uganda
GM bananas **208**.1
withdrawal of aid due to anti-gay laws **225**.14
Ugly Mugs scheme for sex worker protection
246.18, 19
UK **240**.3, 21-2
AIDS strategy support **243**.28
child exploitation **202**.1-2
and children's rights **229**.24, 29-30
climate change impacts **216**.9
climate change targets **216**.33
counter-terrorism strategy **212**.17-18
review **212**.21-2, 38-9

economy **227**.3
endangered species **193**.31-9
energy policy **204**.7-8, 28-9
genetically modified crops **208**.5, 17-18, 25-6
government and politics **240**.21-2, 25-31
HIV/AIDS statistics **243**.2, 5, 14-15
immigration **220**.20-21, 24-5
population diversity **240**.15-16
population goals **220**.19
poverty **235**.1-22
terrorism **212**.4, 5-7, 8-10, 14
and torture complicity **229**.21-3
tourism **222**.1-3, 4-5, 11
trade initiatives **226**.28
trafficked children **202**.27-9, 30, 31
Youth Parliament **240**.38-9
see also entries under British
UN *see* United Nations
unborn babies, effects of domestic abuse **224**.24,
37
underage gambling **203**.12-14
underoccupation
and housing benefit cuts **235**.9
and housing redistribution **253**.17
unemployment **235**.6
black graduates **236**.19-20
ethnic minorities **236**.10-11
older people with HIV **243**.31
as reason for return migration **220**.34
statistics **227**.16
young people **183**.37-8
and mental health **252**.21
UNESCO, education programmes **229**.28
UNICEF
End Child Exploitation campaign **202**.2
projects **229**.24-6
Unilever, advertising **234**.22-3
Union Flag **240**.4-5
unipolar (endogenous) depression **190**.10, 22-3
United Nations (UN)
body image event **234**.37
business and human rights **227**.27, 28
climate change conferences **216**.37, 38, 39
Convention on the Rights of the Child **202**.2;
229.24-6, 29; **248**.35
education programmes **229**.28
encouraging vegan diet **214**.24
Environment Programme (UNEP) **193**.10-11, 13
and human rights of lesbian, gay, bisexual and
transgender people **229**.31-2
Palermo Protocol (prevention of trafficking)
229.17
Population Fund (UNFPA) **229**.28
report on ageing population **239**.13
public attitudes to UN role in human rights **229**.11
REDD rainforest protection programme **218**.20-
21
Strategic Drugs Policy Review **186**.38
units of alcohol **194**.4-5, 14
recommended safe limits **194**.8, 14, 18
Universal Declaration of Human Rights **229**.1
and business **227**.28
universities **209**.27-39

application numbers **209**.37-8
  from state schools **185**.19-20
black students **236**.19-20
business involvement **185**.34-6
climate change emails, University of East Anglia
    216.22
comparing standards **185**.26-8
and ethnic minorities **236**.10, 19-20
and extremism **212**.13-14
funding **209**.29, 31-2, 35
  Youth Parliament manifesto **240**.38
government policy framework **185**.25
paid-for places **219**.30, 36
predictor of degree results **219**.32
reasons for not going to university **185**.16-17;
    209.27, 28
school background of students **185**.19-20
and social class **209**.34-5
and social mobility **185**.18-20
student finance **185**.2; **209**.31-2; **250**.22-5
student life **209**.30-33
university structure reform **185**.20-21
see also degrees; further education; higher
education; students
unreasonable behaviour as grounds for divorce
    244.30, 31
uppers *see* stimulants
urban areas
  and sustainability **218**.6
  sustainable transport networks **200**.30-31
urban extensions **253**.20
urine testing in sport **198**.27
USA
  AIDS strategy support **243**.28
  armed forces and sexual orientation **225**.38-9
  Charter Schools **209**.20
  death penalty **223**.39; **229**.37
  environmental impact **193**.5
  and euthanasia **217**.2, 11
  IVF clinics offering sex selection **247**.36
  online piracy laws **230**.35-6
  privacy rights **245**.4
  religious belief **215**.6
  torture of prisoners by soldiers **212**.36-7

vaccines
  against HPV (cervical cancer) **237**.26-7, 28, 29-31
  benefits of **233**.33
  production from GM plants **208**.21-2
Value Added Tax (VAT) **250**.14
vandalism, racist **236**.14
varioceles and male infertility **247**.2
vascular dementia **201**.10; **239**.28
VAT (Value Added Tax) **250**.14
veganism **214**.1, 2, 3
  and children **214**.28
  and health **214**.37

and heart-related diseases **214**.33
  reasons for **214**.3; **233**.2
  United Nations encouragement of **214**.24
vegetables *see* fruit and vegetables
vegetarian diets **214**.1, 2
vegetarianism **205**.37-8; **214**.1-39
  and children **214**.28, 36
  definition **214**.1, 28
  and the environment **214**.15-27
  and health **214**.5, 12, 28-9, 31-2, 38-9
  history of **214**.4
  and religion **214**.5, 6, 13
  reasons for becoming vegetarian **214**.4-5, 13
  types of vegetarianism **214**.1, 2
Vehicle Excise Duty (car tax) **200**.7
veils, Muslim women **215**.34-9
vending machines, interactive **245**.34-5
vertical occupational segregation **221**.27
veterans *see* ex-service personnel
Veto Violence campaign **240**.35
victimisation **225**.28
  definition **221**.3
  of mental health sufferers **201**.22
  racial **236**.2
victims of bullying **232**.2, 8
  characteristics **232**.2, 8, 31
  effects of bullying **232**.3, 8, 21, 25, 26
  feelings **232**.21, 26
  what to do **232**.18, 26
victims of crime
  mental health sufferers **201**.22
  and restorative justice **223**.29
  role in justice system **223**.24
victims of domestic abuse **224**.2
  disabled people **224**.4
  getting help **224**.38
  LGBT people **224**.5, 12-13
  male **224**.5, 9-10, 11
  older people **224**.4
  pregnant women **224**.4-5
  reasons for not leaving **224**.6
  young people **224**.4, 16-21, 24, 25
  women **224**.2, 3-4, 11
video games, age ratings **196**.17
Video Recordings Act 1984 **196**.14
videos
  cyberbullying **232**.29
  and data protection **232**.35
  see also films
vInspired **240**.35
violence
  against girls **221**.37, 38
  against Muslims **215**.28-30
  against school staff **209**.16
  by children **224**.22-3
  at football grounds **198**.13
  and gangs **223**.6-7, 13-15
  and life on the streets **189**.27-8
  and mental ill health **201**.22, 26
  as obscenity **196**.22
  in pornography **246**.2
  against women **221**.37
    impact of sexual imagery **238**.10-12

men's attitudes **246**.25
see also domestic abuse; physical abuse; sexual abuse
violent crime, trends **223**.4
violent extremism
    condemned by Islam **215**.10
    in schools **212**.12
    in universities **212**.13-14
virtual stores **245**.35
vitamins
    B vitamins **214**.34
    in meat **214**.34
    supplements **205**.4; **214**.10, 29
    and vegetarian diet **205**.38; **214**.28, 29, 30, 33
    vitamin D **214**.34
vivisection *see* animal experimentation
vocational qualifications
    attitudes to **209**.1-3
    at schools **183**.31
    see also specialist diplomas
vocational training and gender **221**.28
Vogue magazine **234**.5-6
voice, children's rights to **229**.25-6
Voice over Internet Protocol (VoIP) **210**.13
void marriages **244**.3
volatile substance abuse *see* solvent abuse
voluntary activity **240**.33-6
    Big Society **240**.33-4
    gap year volunteering **240**.36
    graduates **185**.31
    older people **239**.27
    volunteer tourism **222**.8, 27-8, 36-9
    young people **240**.33-4, 35-6
voluntary euthanasia *see* assisted suicide
vomiting, eating disorders **249**.2
voting
    lowering voting age **240**.30-31, 39
    prisoners' right to vote **229**.35-6
    voting systems **240**.29
    women's right to vote **221**.36
vulnerable employment, developing countries **235**.26
vulnerable people and assisted dying legalization **217**.7-8, 12, 19, 32, 33, 39

wages
    ethnic pay gap **236**.18
    footballers **198**.12
    garment industry **229**.13
    high earners' attitudes to **227**.24-5
    inequality **227**.15, 16
    minimum wage, young people **183**.28
    public perceptions of wage levels **219**.15
    soldiers **213**.1
    see also earnings; incomes; salaries
WAGs (footballers wives and girlfriends) **198**.15-17
waist measurement and health risk **241**.14-15
Wales
    abortion law **231**.3
    drug strategy **228**.24
    empty homes **253**.32
    feelings of Welsh identity **240**.8, 12, 18
    health and physical activity **241**.1-4
    homelessness **189**.4
    National Assembly **240**.27
    plastic bag charge **242**.25
    sports schemes to close poverty gap **241**.29-30
    teenage pregnancy **182**.2, 7, 10-11
walking
    and mental health **252**.26
    to school **200**.7
    see also exercise
war
    as cause of migration **220**.36-7
    and public grief **192**.7-8
Warsi, Baroness Sayeeda **215**.31-2
waste **218**.11-12; **242**.1-39
    electronic **218**.15-16; **242**.20-21
        EU exports **242**.19
    and energy generation **204**.6, 24; **242**.32-3
    export of waste **242**.18-19, 22
        illegal **242**.10, 11-12
        from Norway to Sweden **242**.37
    food **205**.31, 32; **242**.3, 14-16, 38-9
    government policies **242**.1-4, 9
    hazardous **218**.12
        EU trade **242**.18-19
        illegal dumping **242**.10-11
    illegal activities **242**.8-9, 10-12
    incineration **242**.34-6
        plant threatening waste pickers' jobs **242**.29
        producing energy **242**.32-3
        Sweden importing waste for energy plants **242**.37
    landfill **242**.5, 7
    litter **242**.13, 17
    plastic bags **242**.25-7, 28
    reducing waste **218**.11
    see also household waste; landfill; litter; organic waste;
        recycling
Waste-as-Resource(WaR) facilities **242**.33
Waste from Electrical and Electronic Equipment (WEEE) **242**.20-21
waste hierarchy **218**.11; **242**.2
water consumption **205**.27-8
    and the environment **205**.32
    labelling of bottled waters **205**.11
    reducing **218**.34-5
    statistics **218**.36-7
water pollution **218**.38-9
water power **204**.19, 27
water supplies
    and agriculture **214**.17
    and climate change **216**.6, 10
    drinking water access, developing countries **218**.31-3, 36
    freshwater resources **193**.5
    and GM crops **208**.20
    and population growth **220**.6
    scarcity **218**.33
watershed
    for music videos and lyrics **238**.20
    television **238**.5, 20

wave energy **204**.20, 26
wealth
    inherited **219**.8
    and teenage drinking **194**.24
weapons
    gun crime **223**.5
    knife crime *see* knife crime
weather
    events of 2010 **216**.5, 13
    predictions, UK **216**.9
websites
    blocking **196**.38
    newspapers **210**.19
    promoting eating disorders **249**.29-31
    and self-harm **199**.19
weight *see* body weight; obesity
weight loss
    dieting **205**.22-3
    and Quorn **214**.9
    surgery **241**.18, 22
weight problems *see* obesity; underweight people
weisure **183**.19
welfare reform bill **235**.9, 10
welfare support *see* state benefits
West Antarctic ice sheet **216**.12
West Lothian question **240**.28
Western countries *see* developed countries
whales
    animal rights **233**.20, 21
    hunting **193**.1
    impact of climate change **193**.29
    whale watching holidays **222**.26
wheelchairs **197**.11
    wheelchair sport **198**.20-21
white British pupils, poverty and academic
performance **209**.13-14; **219**.29-30
Whitehouse, Mary **196**.25-6
WHO *see* World Health Organisation
WikiLeaks **210**.20-26
wild animals
    in circuses **233**.4, 14-15
    reintroduction in Britain **193**.33-4
wildlife
    butterflies, Britain **193**.36
    impact of chemicals **193**.16-17
    impact of non-native species **193**.12, 38-9
    London **193**.35
    and organic farming **205**.35
    reintroduction of species, Britain **193**.33
    species loss, England **193**.31-2
    tourism **222**.26
    trade **193**.20-21
    see also conservation; endangered species;
extinction
wills **192**.24, 25-7
    living *see* advance directives
wind farms **204**.13-18
    costs **204**.17-18
    impacts on local communities **204**.12
    offshore **204**.14-18
    under-performance **204**.13, 18
wind power **204**.3, 11-18, 25-6; **218**.10
    EU targets **204**.11

    microgeneration **204**.35
    UK targets **204**.8, 17
Windsor and Maidenhead, rewards for recycling
    242.31
Winehouse, Amy
    death prompting call for drugs education
    228.10-11
    suffering from bulimia **249**.24
winter fuel payments **204**.23
witchcraft accusations and child abuse **248**.21-3
withdrawal symptoms, gambling **203**.6
withdrawing medical treatment **217**.14
Wolfenden Committee **246**.17
wolves, reintroduction into Britain **193**.33, 34
women
    and abortion **231**.18-19
        right to choose **231**.17, 25
    and alcohol **194**.7, 14
        pregnant women **194**.14
    and Armed Forces **213**.12-14
    aspiring to be WAGS **198**.15-17
    body image concerns **234**.14-15
    career aspirations **221**.21
    as domestic abuse perpetrators **224**.9-10
    as domestic abuse victims **224**.2, 3-4, 11
    eating disorders **249**.12, 15-16
    and exercise **241**.11-12
    and fertility *see* fertility
    financial implications of partner's death **192**.33
    and gambling
        online gambling **203**.35-6
        as target of gaming companies **203**.26
    gender pay gap **221**.22-5, 27-8, 35-6, 37
    glass ceiling **221**.21-2
    and HIV/AIDS **243**.6
        diagnosis during pregnancy **243**.13
        transmission to baby **243**.1-2, 25
    and household tasks **221**.6
    and inequality **221**.1-2, 33-6, 37
    Internet usage **230**.2-3
    IVF procedure **247**.9-10, 11-12
    marriage expectations **244**.6-7
    maternity leave **183**.18, 21, 23, 24
    media usage **210**.12
    migrant workers **220**.35
    Muslim
        and face veils **215**.34-9
        as victims of hate crime **215**.29
    and the news **210**.6-8
    older women and IVF **247**.10, 22-6
    and politics **221**.2, 13, 15, 20, 36, 37
    and pornography industry **246**.3, 4-5
    post-natal depression **190**.2, 14-15, 21-2
    pregnant women
        dietary supplements **205**.4
        eating disorders **249**.12
        and smoking **188**.11, 30-32
    prisoners, self-harm **199**.12
    effects of prostitution **246**.19-20, 27-8
    and provocative clothing **221**.12
    rights, global public attitudes **229**.12
    sexualisation, compliance in **238**.36-8
    and sexually transmitted infections (STIs) **237**.4,

19, 22
shopaholism **207**.6
and smoking **188**.1, 3, 15
  in pregnancy **188**.11, 30-32
and stress **206**.8-9
voting rights **221**.36
working hours and divorce **244**.33
see also girls and young women; mothers;
pregnancy; working mothers
women in the workforce
  effect of children on career **183**.21
  equal pay *see* gender pay gap
  glass ceiling **221**.21-2
  mothers preferring not to work **183**.25
  in senior positions **183**.12; **221**.13-22
  see also working mothers
wood fuelled heating **204**.36
wood waste trade, EU **242**.18
work
  effects of cannabis use **186**.10
  effect on fathers' involvement with children
    191.33
  effect of money worries **250**.33
  and homelessness **189**.33
    Big Issue selling **189**.37-9
  in prison **223**.23
  past retirement age **239**.16, 18
  workers' rights **229**.14-16
  see also child labour; employment; migrant
workers
work and gender *see* gender and work
work-family balance, fathers **191**.34-5
work-life balance **183**.16-17, 22-3
  see also hours of work
Work Positive **206**.26
work-related stress **183**.6-7; **206**.7-9, 17-18, 24-9
  causes **206**.29
  costs **183**.6-7; **206**.5
  legislation **206**.25, 28-9
  signs **206**.7-9
working class, prejudice against **219**.3-6
working conditions, developing countries
  garment industry, campaign for living wage
    229.13
  improvement initiatives **226**.28
working hours *see* hours of work
working mothers **191**.36
  effects on children **221**.26
  maternity rights **191**.37-8
  preferring not to work **183**.25
working parents **191**.30-39
  and stress **206**.22-3
workplace
  absences **183**.8, 9
  age discrimination **239**.6, 12-13
  and disabled people **197**.20-21, 24-5, 26-7
  drug misuse signs **228**.15
  gender balance **221**.19
  sexual orientation discrimination **225**.9, 28-9
  stress *see* work-related stress
workplace bullying **232**.23, 24
  cyberbullying **227**.38
workplace pensions **250**.12

World Bank **226**.9-10
  and gender equality **221**.2
  and poverty reduction **235**.23-4, 32
World Health Organization
  criticism of homeopathy **195**.30-31
  mental health programmes **201**.8-9
world trade *see* international trade
World Trade Organization (WTO) **226**.1, 7-8, 14-15
  criticism of **226**.14-15, 32
  trade rules **226**.27

Y

Yemen, death penalty **229**.37
YMCA, homelessness projects **189**.22
young carers **201**.8-9
  mental health problems **201**.4
  and neglect **248**.15
young children
  eating disorders **249**.3, 7-8, 22
  sexualisation of girls **221**.9-10
Young Life and Times survey (Northern Ireland)
    237.15-17
young offenders
  maturity as a factor in sentencing **223**.33-4
  and prison **223**.28-9
young onset dementia **201**.10-11
young parents **182**.14-18
  housing rights **189**.25
young people
  and age discrimination **239**.6
  in the Armed Forces **213**.15-16
  attitudes to ageing **239**.6-7
  attitudes to higher education **209**.27-8
  attitudes to riots **223**.9, 10-11
  and bariatric surgery **241**.22
  and body image **234**.7, 26
  and cannabis
    anti-drug helpline criticised **186**.26-7
    effect on families **186**.23-5
    mental health effects **186**.10, 29
    penalties for possession **186**.1-2, 5, 9, 30
    worldwide use **186**.19
  caring for parents with mental health problems
    201.8-9
  and contraceptive information **237**.8-9
  and cosmetic surgery **234**.33, 34
  and crime *see* young offenders; youth crime
  and criminal justice system **223**.25
    maturity as a factor in sentencing **223**.33-4
  and cyberbullying **232**.30-32
  and depression **190**.25-30
  digital fluency **230**.10-12
  and disability **197**.16-17, 36-7
  and domestic abuse **224**.16-26
    effects of domestic abuse **224**.24-5
    teenage relationship abuse **224**.4, 16-21, 35-6
  and drug abuse **228**.1; **252**.1, 31, 32, 35
    treatment **228**.17
  education on HIV/AIDS **243**.10-11
  entrepreneurial aspirations **227**.6

financial skills **250**.17, 18
and gambling **203**.9-18
    Internet gambling **203**.16-18
    problem gambling **203**.9-10, 12, 15, 16, 20
    reasons for gambling **203**.9
gang membership **189**.28; **223**.6-7, 13-15
girls in prostitution **246**.27-8, 34-8
and grief **192**.9-23
health **252**.1-12
    and happiness **241**.8
and HIV/AIDS **243**.10-11, 23-5
and home ownership **253**.2-3, 4
homelessness **189**.21-32
    statistics **189**.21, 23
housing rights **189**.24-5
HPV (cervical cancer) vaccination **237**.27, 28, 29- 31
and identity fraud risk **245**.21-2
and the Internet **230**.4-5, 8-13, 33-4
leaving home, reasons **189**.24, 25, 26, 27
and marriage **244**.1
media usage **210**.5, 11
and mental health **190**.27; **252**.13-26
and mental health problems **201**.2-4, 29-30
and mental health services **201**.36
men using prostitutes **246**.24
mentoring by ex-service personnel **213**.32
and modelling **234**.35
and money **250**.17-28
not in employment, education or training (NEET) **183**.32
parenthood *see* teenage parents
physical activity guidelines **241**.6
and pornography **238**.3-4; **246**.10-11, 12, 13
and pregnancy *see* teenage pregnancies
savings **250**.26, 27-8, 36
and self-harm **252**.22-3
sexual behaviour **237**.15-17
and sexual orientation **225**.1, 2-3, 5-8
and sexually transmitted infections (STIs) **237**.10,   23, 24-5; **252**.2, 3
and sexual violence **238**.15
sleep deprivation and mental health **201**.7
and smoking **188**.24-8; **252**.1-2, 31, 35, 37-9
    stopping smoking **188**.13-14
and social mobility **219**.18
and suicide **199**.21, 28, 31-3
unemployment **183**.37-8
and vegetarian diet **214**.36
and volunteering **240**.33-4, 35-6
and work **183**.28-39
    difficulties finding work **183**.30
    problems at work **183**.30-31
young people and alcohol **194**.1-3, 24, 25-6
alcohol consumption **194**.1-2; **252**.2, 31, 35
binge drinking **252**.36
drinking behaviour **194**.2-3, 24, 25
influence of household drinking habits **194**.25
influence of sports stars drinking **198**.14
obtaining alcohol **194**.3
reasons for drinking **194**.3
risks **194**.19-20
Young Person's Development Programme (YPDP)

182.30
Youngminds **252**.15
Youth Career Initiative (tourism industry) **222**.31
youth crime
    and gangs **223**.6-7, 13-15
    prevention, role of ex-offenders **223**.18
    see also young offenders
youth justice **223**.25, 31
Youth Parliament **240**.38-9
YouTube
    and body image **234**.9
    reporting inappropriate content **232**.36
Yuckies (Young Unwitting Costly Kids) **191**.27-8

Z

Zambia, income growth **235**.29
Zero Exclusion Pilot programme **213**.32
zero waste economy **242**.3
zinc in diet **214**.34
Zombies, Run! fitness app **241**.38
zoos
    and animal welfare **233**.24-5
    and conservation **233**.25

Vol. numbers appear first (in bold) followed by page numbers; a change in volume is preceded by a semi-colon. You can also find this title list at the front of the book.